THE GRANULARITY OF GROWTH: ASIA

HOW TO DRIVE GROWTH IN THE WORLD'S MOST DYNAMIC ECONOMIES

ANGUS DAWSON WITH JONATHAN AUERBACH, WONSIK CHOI,
CARL HARRIS, KULDEEP JAIN, PETER KENEVAN, SANGBEOM KIM,
GORDON ORR, VIVEK PANDIT, HERBERT POHL & ADIL ZAINULBHAI

CYAN

Marshall Cavendish
Business

Copyright © 2007 McKinsey & Company Inc. United States

First published in 2007 by:

Marshall Cavendish Limited
Fifth Floor
32–38 Saffron Hill
London EC1N 8FH
United Kingdom
T: +44 (0)20 7421 8120
F: +44 (0)20 7421 8121
sales@marshallcavendish.co.uk
www.marshallcavendish.co.uk

and

Cyan Communications Limited
Fifth Floor
32–38 Saffron Hill
London EC1N 8FH
United Kingdom
T: +44 (0)20 7421 8145
T: +44 (0)20 7421 8146
sales@cyanbooks.com
www.cyanbooks.com

The right of Jonathan Auerbach, Wonsik Choi, Angus Dawson,
Carl Harris, Kuldeep Jain, Peter Kenevan, Sangbeom Kim,
Gordon Orr, Vivek Pandit, Herbert Pohl, and Adil Zainulbhai to
be identified as the authors of this work has been asserted by them
in accordance with the Copyright, Designs and Patents Act 1988.

A CIP record for this book is available from the
British Library.

ISBN-13 978-1-905736-38-6
ISBN-10 1-905736-38-X

Typeset by Phoenix Photosetting, Chatham, Kent
www.phoenixphotosetting.co.uk

Printed and bound in Great Britain by
Mackays of Chatham Limited, Chatham, Kent

Contents

Acknowledgements

The Granularity of Growth: Asia is the result of a team effort that goes well beyond its eleven authors. The writing of this book has been a powerful catalyst for building a real growth community of clients and colleagues in Asia – one that includes the business leaders in the region who have put growth at the top of their operational agenda as well as members of McKinsey's Asia-Pacific and Middle East strategy and corporate finance practices.

In particular, we are grateful for the research carried out by Megha Aggarwal, Ankit Ahuja, Gautam Bakshi, Ripsy Bakshi, Neha Behl, Sindy Chen, Nuo Dai, Chintan Dhebar, Sumit Dora, Yamini Garg, Satish K. Gupta, Himanshu Jain, Namit Jain, Amit Jeffrey, Wenyi Jin, Kamaruzaman Kamarudin, Vipin Karnani, Kyungye Kim, Adrian Lim, Lydia Lu, Rohit Malhotra, Amit Marwah, Devesh Mittal, Gauri Nagraj, Bhawna Prakash, Manpreet Randhawa, Sudipto Roy, Amit H. Sharma, Ashish Sharma, Siddhartha Sharma, Cliff Shi, Vivek Sikaria, Arjun Singh, Maninder Singh, Richa Suri, James Tang, Jiajun Wu, Derek Xu, and Yanyan Xu.

The inspiration and foundation for this book comes from *The Granularity of Growth* and its authors, Patrick Viguerie, Sven Smit, and Mehrdad Baghai. In addition, many of our colleagues in Asia-Pacific and the Middle East have contributed to individual chapters, providing additional research or challenging our views. They include Adam Lewis, Jessica Morgan, and Ralph Wiechers (Australia); Andrew Grant and Xiaoyu Xia (China); Kito de Boer, Amadeo Di Lodovico, Armin Lohr, Laurent Nordin, Hans-Martin Stockmeier, John Tiefel, and Ahmed Yahia (the Gulf Cooperation Council); Noshir Kaka, Gautam Kumra, Joydeep Sengupta, Ramdoss Seetharaman, and Toshan Tamhane (India); Heang Chhor and Nozomu Masuyama (Japan); Diaan-Yi Lin, Badrinath Ramanathan, and Peter Schoppert (Southeast Asia); and Stephen Bear, Kevin Kim, and Roland Villinger (Korea). We are also grateful for the support provided by Dominic Barton. Despite all their excellent help and advice, none of these individuals are accountable for what follows. Their support has been invaluable, but any flaws contained in these pages rest entirely with the authors. Similarly, the opinions expressed here are strictly our own.

This book has come to fruition thanks to the support, insight, and perseverance of Claudia Sandoval Parra and Pranav Shirke, who managed it through its creation and worked with the authors and researchers to develop each chapter. Without them, there would be no book.

We also express our gratitude to Ivan Hutnik for editing the book and to Jacquie Molloy and Patricia Welch for helping to make the chapters more engaging and easy to read.

Finally, we would like to thank Pom Somkabcharti and Martin Liu of Cyan Books for the opportunity to share this information with you, our readers. May your businesses grow . . . and grow . . . and grow.

Angus Dawson on behalf of the authors
Sydney, October 2007

Preface

Growth is a universal management preoccupation, as a glance at shelf after shelf of business books will demonstrate. A new book, *The Granularity of Growth* by Patrick Viguerie, Sven Smit, and Mehrdad Baghai (Cyan/Marshall Cavendish, 2007), sets out to offer an innovative perspective that challenges conventional wisdom on growth. It draws on insights gleaned from McKinsey & Company's comprehensive proprietary database of large companies across the globe and our experience of serving some of the world's most important, dynamic, and fast-growing organizations.

Although the research base of the book is global, its focus falls necessarily on the developed markets, since it is they that have the most accurate data available over the longest time span. All the same, we believe that the book's core insights are highly relevant for companies in Asia. In our work with clients across the region, we have become fascinated by the subtle contextual differences and important nuances in the individual Asian markets. Understanding these nuances is critical for companies in thinking about growth in the region, whether from a local company perspective or from a global one. It was to bring this texture to light that *The Granularity of Growth: Asia* was born.

We have taken a somewhat idiosyncratic view of Asia, analyzing China, India, Japan, and South Korea separately but treating Southeast Asia as one big market rather than a cluster of smaller ones. In terms of scope, we have stretched to the antipodes and included Australia – economically closer to North America and Europe than to Asia – as well as the Gulf States in the west, which are quickly becoming critical trading and financial partners in Asia's growth as well as important markets in their own right.

This book contains one chapter for each of the countries and regions we have analyzed: Australia, China, the Gulf Cooperation Council (GCC), India, Japan, Southeast Asia, and South Korea. Each chapter focuses on the most important contextual elements and local nuances as well as covering the macroeconomic climate, the sources of growth, the companies that have grown strongly to date, and our views on opportunities for growth in the future. We hope our perspective will shape your thinking on growth in the region and help ensure that your company's growth strategies are based on strong fundamentals.

In writing this book, we have assumed that the reader has some familiarity with *The Granularity of Growth*. However, we have included a brief definition of terms and a summary of the main ideas in the introduction, though neither should be taken as a substitute for a granular understanding of the original.

A definition of terms

Growth: an increase in top-line revenues obtained either organically or through acquisitions, either within or outside the core business. Over time, revenue and its development trajectory provide a good (though not perfect) indication of a company's role, influence, leadership, and standing in its markets. In the long term, sustained positive revenue growth is highly correlated with superior value creation.

Granularity: the size of the components within a larger system. We have borrowed this term from science because we believe that winning growth strategies emerge from a much finer than usual – or more "granular" – understanding of market segments, their needs, and the capabilities required to serve them well.

Granular growth decomposition: an analytical method for breaking down the sources of a company's or an industry's growth into the three separate components of portfolio momentum, M&A, and market-share gains.[1]

Tailwind: a favorable market that is growing rapidly, enabling companies to grow through the sheer momentum of their portfolio, independently of any gains they may make in market share or via acquisitions.

The growth performance matrix: a tool for assessing the performance of a sample of companies by dividing them into groups according to their growth in two dimensions: value creation or total returns to shareholders (TRS), using the local market index as the yardstick, and revenue growth, using the national GDP growth rate as the yardstick. The analysis yields four categories:

- *Growth giants:* companies that outperformed the market in TRS and grew their revenues at above the rate of GDP growth.

- *Performers:* companies that outperformed in TRS but lagged in revenue growth.

- *Unrewarded:* companies that lagged in TRS but outperformed in revenue growth.

- *Challenged:* companies that lagged in both TRS and revenue growth.

The growth performance matrix

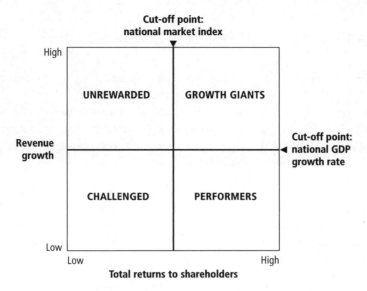

Cut-off point:
national market index

High

| UNREWARDED | GROWTH GIANTS |

Revenue
growth

Cut-off point:
◄ **national GDP**
growth rate

| CHALLENGED | PERFORMERS |

Low

Low   High

Total returns to shareholders

NOTE

[1] For a detailed explanation, see chapter 2 of *The Granularity of Growth.*

Introduction

GROWTH HAS NEVER REALLY disappeared from the CEO's agenda, and nowhere is this more true than in Asia. In the past ten years, we have seen the rise of the growth powerhouses of China and India, Australia topping the OECD growth list, and the emergence of the Gulf States as new regional economic powers. Over the same period, CEOs in markets such as Japan, South Korea, and Southeast Asia have focused on operational enhancements to boost their performance and earn the right to survive.

The past decade has been one of contrasts in Asia: a time of exceptional growth, but also one of trauma. Markets have been reshaped, whether in response to macroeconomic downturns or to unlock further growth potential. Openness has increased. Governments have started to deregulate their economies, opening up predominantly state-owned sectors to private and foreign investment. And in the wake of the Asian financial crisis of 1997, this has also been a time of reassessment.

Throughout all these upheavals, the big economies have followed their own separate paths. India has continued down the path of slow deregulation that it started in 1991, while China's initial steps to embrace market mechanisms marked the beginning of a journey of stunning economic transformation.

Now, after a decade of repair and reinvention in some markets and spectacular growth and wealth creation in others, the focus is squarely on growth. No CEO or board can afford to neglect the key questions: where will the next big wave of growth come from? What new challenges will it bring? How will our company tackle them?

The Granularity of Growth: Asia is a call to arms for every executive in the region to develop a broad yet fine-grained vision about where their company's growth will come from, and to design the strategy and organization needed to make it happen. As well as providing an analytical and conceptual foundation for this process, we offer practical examples and insights to inform – and, we hope, inspire – business leaders who are rising to the challenge of crafting their own growth strategies.

The challenge of growth

To uncover opportunities for growth, executives need to dig deep into their organization – something that many have been unable or unwilling to do in the past. Even those companies that know how to manage their operations in minute detail often continue to handle strategic choices at a high level. The challenge they face is to find a way to make these choices at a finer, more *granular* level without losing focus or drowning in a sea of complexity.

The growth challenge has two aspects: the challenge of size and the challenge of longevity. As for *size*, the bigger you are, the harder it is to achieve the next quantum of growth. As for *longevity*, the longer you have been in business, the more likely you are to need to rejuvenate your business, break out of organizational inertia, and make new efforts to keep in touch with evolving customer needs, new competitors, and new business models. Companies facing both or either of these challenges need to unleash granular opportunities wherever they may be.

Four big ideas
The Granularity of Growth sets out four big ideas that all business leaders should heed whether they are in developing or developed economies and irrespective of company size, business model, and geographic spread:

- **Grow or go.** CEOs and boards need to make a clear choice between realizing value through profitable revenue growth or maximizing value within a low-growth future. Undoubtedly, growth is appealing; after all, it is responsible for driving long-term performance and survival. But ending up stuck in the middle between growth and aggressive value maximization is likely to lead to underperformance and, in countries where capital markets are well developed, to being acquired.

- **Granularity.** Growth is granular: it involves getting beyond the aggregates and averages to a more fine-grained view of your growth sources, your markets, and your capabilities. Management teams need to change the way they think about their markets. Don't think about your two or three main markets; think about the hundred or more sub-markets you are in and whether you have the insights – and the organization model – to achieve growth in them.

- **Where to compete.** Sustained revenue growth isn't really about the "how to compete" actions that companies take to improve their execution and market share. It comes much more from "where to compete" choices such as "Which market do we focus on?" and "Which company should we buy?" This is not to say that CEOs should relax their focus on ensuring they are better at executing than their competitors, only to warn that very few companies manage to change their growth trajectory over time simply by making market-share gains. In developed economies, the market growth rates of the businesses you are in and your M&A activity are *four times more important* than changes in market share in explaining revenue growth.

- **Architecture.** Designing and executing strategies at a granular level challenges traditional notions of strategy development and organization design, including the way you think about scale platforms and management processes. Developing a comprehensive organizational architecture for growth is fundamental to sustaining profitable growth.

Asian themes

These four ideas need to underpin growth strategies in Asia as much as anywhere else. In addition, we have identified four important cross-cutting themes that are specific to the region, and vital for its management teams to consider.

Shifting patterns of demand

Much is made of the impressive overall growth rates of the Asian economies, and rightly so. However, if we probe beneath these aggregate numbers, stark differences emerge in individual markets' growth and attractiveness. This has important implications for executives pursuing growth. Strategies that strive to capture small shares of big, fast-growing markets are dangerous because the *real* shifts in demand tend to happen at the much more granular level of customer segments, product categories, and geographic markets.

As new middle classes emerge, new product categories such as ultra-cheap cars are being created to serve them, along with services that need to be economic with much smaller revenue streams than in developed markets. However, the pace at which these markets emerge and grow is not uniform; steady growth is often followed by a sudden explosive spurt like those seen in China's software and automobile sectors. Though luck plays a part, the companies that have succeeded in capturing such growth are those that have made in-depth granular assessments to establish which market segments are attractive and when is the best time to enter them.

In much the same way, the large-scale shifts in demand that are in the process of reshaping value in many markets need to be understood at a granular level, not a macro level, if companies are to appreciate the real nature of the challenges and opportunities that are opening up. Take, for instance, the aging of the population, a demographic shift that is particularly important for the economies of Japan and South Korea. Its effects are complex, and need to be analyzed at the level of individual product categories and customer segments. On the one hand, older people tend to consume much less than younger ones, which means that some product markets such as clothing, furniture, and sports goods may experience a drop in demand; on the other hand, new demands emerge and need to be fulfilled: welfare and pensions, healthcare and health insurance, leisure and travel services.

The need for new business and organization models

Companies that succeed in the Asian environment are flexible, patient, and adaptable. Their cost and pricing models must allow them to serve a single segment across several regions or countries, or several segments within a single country. These models need to incorporate best practices in production and distribution, accommodate discriminatory pricing, and include a framework to enable relationship building and stakeholder management. The focus of such a framework may be on government relationships (as in China, GCC, India, and Southeast Asia); on relationships with family-owned conglomerates (as in GCC, India, Southeast Asia, and South Korea); or on public relations (as in the case of Australia, Southeast Asia, Japan, and South Korea).

Given that the disposable income of the new middle classes in key Asian markets is lower than in developed markets in nominal terms, companies need to serve these consumers in more innovative ways by creating affordable products tailored to individual markets, such as pre-paid mobile telephony services at less than US$1 per top-up.

Another important element to consider when building a business model is the need to tolerate and exploit volatility. As history shows, the Asian economies are among the most dynamic – and thus most volatile – in the world, with rapid growth and rapid consolidation, rapid descent into crisis and rapid recovery from it, rapidly emerging new business opportunities and rapid change in the size of these opportunities and their associated profit pools. The key is to produce flexible yet resilient organizations that are capable of riding the tailwinds of rapid growth successfully.

Companies need the restraint to wait and then the courage and ability to scale up rapidly as markets explode. The companies exploiting the multimillion-dollar opportunities that have emerged in Asia over the past decade have needed more patience than is usually required in developed economies, as well as a business model with processes, systems, and talent that can be rapidly scaled up with the utmost control and discipline. The family ownership model that still prevails in many Asian markets seems, in many instances, to have been capable of meeting both these challenges.

The increasing maturity of capital markets

One of the positive outcomes of the financial crisis of the late 1990s was the recognition that the development of a sound capital market was crucial to recovery. Though the level of development varies from one Asian market to another, all of the economies now have fully functioning capital markets. More and more, these markets are providing the necessary funding for growth and creating discipline in companies' governance, transparency, and reporting, as we see in the Southeast Asia, India, and GCC chapters.

Another manifestation of this change in capital markets is the emergence of a mindset geared to investing rather than saving. Individuals, corporations, and governments are starting to take managed risks, which is opening up new sources of funding. This shift has also led to the emergence of new entities that are virtually private-equity firms, except with a twist: they are linked to government. As a result, they are able to invest part of their government's foreign-currency reserves, as well as their populations' pension funds, as in Singapore. In some countries, these entities are also able to take advantage of higher commodity prices (be it in petroleum, iron ore, or copper) and to invest the additional revenues their countries receive. We look at these government-linked investment companies in the GCC and Southeast Asia chapters.

The third consequence of the development of capital markets is that it creates scope for consolidation at both the market and regional level. Although regulatory barriers and local cultural norms governing the way business is conducted mean that M&A is still far from common, most Asian countries have experienced a few mergers and acquisitions. Early movers are demonstrating that it is possible to build new capabilities that allow effective cross-border M&A, and in so doing they are becoming an inspiration for aspiring multinationals. They have paved the way in creating new models for governance; the recruitment, development, and management of global talent; the two-way transfer of know-how; and the management of capital-market and private-equity funding.

The continuing role of government

The role of the government remains important in Asian economies and should never be overlooked when companies are scanning "where to compete" opportunities and deciding how to capture them. State-owned enterprises

(SOEs) account for a significant part of the economy in most markets and represent important competitors as well as customers. Even in countries where industries have been liberalized, government restrictions on foreign ownership, foreign direct investment, and M&A persist, affecting business opportunities and the way business is conducted. But not all the news is bad. The emergence of government-linked investment companies in several industries is not only creating strong competitors, but also facilitating joint ventures and funding.

In addition, some governments are starting to manage their economy as if it were a company. We can see this already in Singapore, Malaysia, and Dubai, and it looks likely to happen in China too. Government purchases are treated as corporate purchases, and fiscal and monetary policies are managed in the same way as a company's treasury. However, these governments are still maintaining subsidies and welfare measures to support poor citizens, particularly in countries where migrants workers make up an important part of the economy. As with companies, profits are channelled back into investment so as to allow the countries concerned to exploit further business opportunities.

Relationships with the regional, state, and national governments have always been at the core of business etiquette and reputation building in Asia. While corporate governance is becoming more transparent, objective, and independent, this represents a radically new way of working for these countries, and it would be unreasonable to expect the culture of transacting business to change overnight. As in developed markets, it is always wise to seize any opportunity to build relationships of trust with policy makers and advisers.

■ ■ ■

Growth is a constant battle, not only to survive but to become bigger and better. We hope that *The Granularity of Growth: Asia* will shed light on the nature of the challenge and help companies make decisions that will lead to enduring performance.

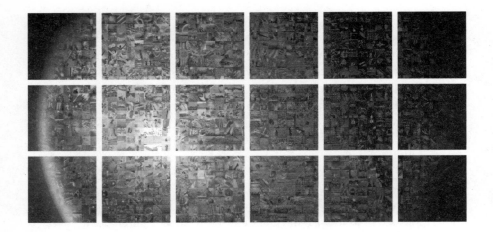

1

Australia: Now the lucky need to prove they are good

Angus Dawson

SINCE THE END OF THE RECESSION of the early 1990s, Australia has enjoyed one of the greatest periods of economic prosperity in its history. The facts speak for themselves. The overall economy grew at a compound annual growth rate (CAGR) of 3.7 percent, compared to 3.2 percent in the US and an OECD average of 2.4 percent.[1] Australia's All Ordinaries share index rose at 9.5 percent, not far off the 10.1 percent increase in the S&P 500 in the US.[2]

The foundations for this prosperity were laid in the 1980s, with far-reaching measures that included the dismantling of tariff protections and exchange-rate controls, the beginning of the reform of the tax system, and a steady stream of privatizations. The trend continued into the 1990s and the first half of the present decade in the form of further tax reform, more privatizations, the deregulation of labor markets, and increased fiscal discipline, assisted by a massive China-led resources boom.

Australia's corporate landscape now looks very different to that of fifteen years ago. The companies that grew have mostly thrived. Conversely, many of those that failed to grow no longer exist as independent entities.

How companies fared

To gain more insight into what these companies did and how it influenced their fate, we looked at their performance in terms of revenue and total returns to shareholders (TRS) over time. To do this, we took Australia's largest companies at the end of the 1980s and tracked their fortunes up to the present. Our sample consisted of 86 companies that appeared in both the list of the 100 biggest companies by market value and the list of the 100 biggest companies by revenue.

First we examined what happened to these companies over the first business cycle from 1989 to 1995, and then we followed them through the second cycle from 1995 to 2005. As in the analysis described in the Introduction of *The Granularity of Growth*, we sorted the companies by whether they grew revenue at above or below the nominal GDP growth rate and whether their total returns to shareholders (TRS) were above or below the market average as measured by the ASX200.

In the first cycle, 1989 to 1995, nominal GDP grew by an average of 4 percent, and the ASX200 TRS grew at an average of 12 percent. By the end of the cycle, 23 out of our sample of 86 companies qualified as *growth giants*, 8 were *performers*, 24 were *unrewarded*, and 31 were *challenged* (Figure 1.1). So

1.1 The growth performance matrix

Share of sample* by category based on performance in cycle 1 (1989–95), percent

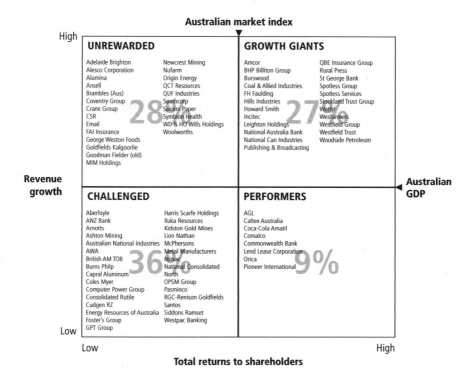

* 86 companies that appear in both the list of top 100 companies by revenues and the list of top 100 companies by market capitalization
Source: Research Insight; Bloomberg; Datastream; McKinsey analysis

there were almost three times as many growth giants as performers. Put another way, companies that outperformed on TRS were three times more likely to have grown revenue at a rate above GDP than below it.

During the next cycle, nominal GDP grew at a compound average growth rate of 6 percent and the ASX200 TRS grew at 13 percent. When we look at what happened to the four groups of companies during this period, we see some interesting patterns. The *growth giants* displayed remarkable resilience, with 14 out of 23 continuing both to grow revenue at above the rate of GDP and to outperform the stock-market average (Figure 1.2). A similar performance pattern can be seen in other markets including the US, Taiwan, and Japan.

1.2 The growth giants
How they fared in the second cycle

Cycle 1: 1989–1995
Percent of total sample

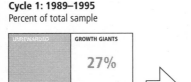

UNREWARDED	GROWTH GIANTS
	27%
CHALLENGED	PERFORMERS

Cycle 2: 1995–2005
Percent of cycle 1 growth giants

UNREWARDED	GROWTH GIANTS
0%	BHP Billiton Group — Wesfarmers Coal & Allied Industries — Westfield Group Hills Industries — Woodside Petroleum Leighton Holdings National Australia Bank Publishing & Broadcasting — 40% QBE Insurance Group Rural Press St George Bank Spotless Group Stockland Trust Group
CHALLENGED Amcor National Can Industries Wattyl 13%	**PERFORMERS** 0%

EXIT
Burswood — Incitec FH Faulding — Spotless Services Howard Smith — Westfield Trust

Source: Research Insight; Bloomberg; Datastream; McKinsey analysis

However, the other three categories don't exhibit such stability. None of the *performers* stayed in that category and continued to outperform the market in terms of TRS (Figure 1.3). Again, this is consistent with their showing in other markets, where they eventually run out of productivity improvements with which to surprise the market positively. In the second cycle, a few performers worked out how to grow and become growth giants, but most suffered a dip in their performance or were acquired.

For both the *challenged* (Figure 1.4) and the *unrewarded* (Figure 1.5) companies, being acquired was the most common fate. Those that remained independent tended not to stay where they were but instead underwent a

1.3 The performers
How they fared in the second cycle

Cycle 1: 1989–1995
Percent of total sample

Cycle 2: 1995–2005
Percent of cycle 1 performers

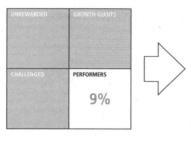

UNREWARDED	GROWTH GIANTS
Lend Lease Corp	AGL Caltex Australia Commonwealth Bank
12%	38%

CHALLENGED	PERFORMERS
Coca-Cola Amatil Orica	
25%	0%

EXIT
Comalco Pioneer International 25%

Source: Research Insight; Bloomberg; Datastream; McKinsey analysis

transformation to become either a growth giant (like Westpac) or a performer (like Lion Nathan).

In fact, Australia saw the highest rate of consolidation of any market we examined. More than half of the companies that failed to grow above GDP during the first business cycle were acquired in the second; the comparable share in the US was much lower, at less than a quarter. This phenomenon was the result of a unique period in the Australian economy in which deregulation, the scale benefits of technology investments, low interest rates, and a national competition policy all combined to promote acquisition.

1.4 The challenged
How they fared in the second cycle

Cycle 1: 1989–1995
Percent of total sample

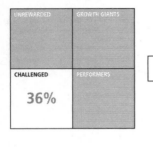

UNREWARDED	GROWTH GIANTS
CHALLENGED	PERFORMERS
36%	

Cycle 2: 1995–2005
Percent of cycle 1 challenged

UNREWARDED	GROWTH GIANTS
0%	ANZ Bank Coles Myer Energy Resources of Australia GPT Group Iluka Resources Santos Westpac Banking 22%

CHALLENGED	PERFORMERS
Burns Philp Capral Aluminum Consolidated Rutile 10%	Foster's Group Lion Nathan McPhersons 10%

EXIT

Aberfoyle	Kidston Gold Mines
Arnotts	Metal Manufacturers
Ashton Mining	Mayne
Australian National Inds	National Consolidated
AWA	North
British AM TOB	OPSM Group
Computer Power Group	Pasminco
Cudgen RZ	RGC-Renison Goldfields
Harris Scarfe Holdings	Siddons Ramset

58%

Source: Research Insight; Bloomberg; Datastream; McKinsey analysis

Once ownership or state regulatory barriers have been removed, the natural end game for most Australian industries is that the sector consolidates, leaving a few national players where once had been a multitude of state-based players. These barriers included mutual or co-operative structures such as those prevalent in the insurance industry; government ownership, once prevalent in the banking industry; or restrictions on ownership that limit takeovers. The removal of these barriers creates entities with a greater ability to raise capital and produces compelling benefits of scale and market concentration. Industries that were fragmented at the state level are now highly concentrated even by global standards, as we see in retail, logistics, banking,

1.5 The unrewarded

How they fared in the second cycle

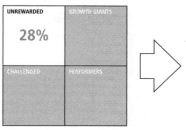

Cycle 1: 1989–1995
Percent of total sample

UNREWARDED	GROWTH GIANTS
28%	
CHALLENGED	PERFORMERS

Cycle 2: 1995–2005
Percent of cycle 1 unrewarded

UNREWARDED	GROWTH GIANTS
Adelaide Brighton Coventry Group Crane Group 13%	Alesco Corporation Brambles (Aus) Nufarm Woolworth's 17%
CHALLENGED	PERFORMERS
Alumina Ansell Symbion Health 13%	CSR Newcrest Mining Origin Energy 13%

EXIT
Email   QCT Resources FAI Insurance   QUF Industries George Weston Foods   Southcorp Goldfields Kalgoorlie   Spicers Paper Goodman Fielder (old)   WD & HO Wills Holdings MIM Holdings 44%

Source: Research Insight; Bloomberg; Datastream; McKinsey analysis

steel, packaging, and consumer goods such as biscuits, snacks, carbonated beverages, beer, and wine.

Where does the growth come from?

When we look at the companies that qualified as growth giants either across both business cycles or only in the second cycle, one thing that stands out is the dominance of a few sectors. All four of the big banks, as well as next-largest St George, are there for the 1995 to 2005 period. Property fares well, as does the resources sector. This was a good period for retailers too, with Woolworths and Coles Myer making the cut. On the other hand, some of their suppliers, such as CCA, Foster's, and Lion Nathan, struggled to deliver above-GDP growth, and many others did not survive the period as independent entities.

We can shed more light on this by using our granular growth decomposition[3] to find out how much of companies' growth came from portfolio momentum, M&A, and market-share gain. By using published data for individual companies, and third-party sources for market growth rates, we can make reasonable estimates, although we can't reach the level of granularity that we get to when we work with clients and have access to their own data. Our database comprises 38 of Australia's largest companies – not necessarily the growth giants that we tracked from the 1980s as explained above, but the top companies in the key sectors where we could obtain reasonable external data to do the analysis. The results of our granular growth decomposition are shown in Figure 1.6, which shows the absolute growth rate over the past five to seven years for companies grouped by sector and how that growth was split between portfolio momentum, M&A, and market-share gains.

Our key finding is that, just as we found when we analyzed our global database as described in *The Granularity of Growth*, M&A and portfolio momentum are much more important than market-share gain in determining both the *absolute* growth rates and the *differences* between company growth rates in nearly every sector. On average, *all* the companies in our Australian database grew at 13.1 percent: 7.8 percent of this was derived from portfolio momentum, 4.6 percent from M&A, and 0.7 percent from market-share gain. Let's look at a couple of sectors in more detail.

In the money

Financial services companies have enjoyed a tremendous tailwind (strong market growth) for the past 15 years. With a strong economy and low interest rates, double-digit credit growth became the norm as housing prices soared and mortgage balances with them. Though margins were squeezed as attackers such as Aussie joined in, that didn't offset the rapid growth in demand.

As Figure 1.6 shows, the granular growth decomposition reveals that the average big bank grew at about 10 percent. There was little difference between individual institutions. Both separately and as a group they conceded small amounts of market share to smaller competitors, but compensated with acquisitions in the insurance and wealth management sectors. Admittedly, market share fluctuated year on year, segment by segment, as one bank improved its execution over another, but any advantage proved temporary

1.6 Drugs of growth

Percent

	Portfolio momentum	M&A	Share gain/loss	Total growth
Banks ANZ CBA NAB	St George Westpac			
Insurance IAG Promina	QBE Suncorp			
Consumer goods Burns Philp Coca-Cola Amatil	Foster's Group Lion Nathan			
Retail Coles Myer Harvey Norman	Wesfarmers Woolworths			
Media and entertainment APN Aristocrat Fairfax PBL	Seven News Tabcorp WAN			
Electricity, oil and gas AGL Alinta Caltex	Origin Santos Woodside			
Basic materials BHP Billiton Bluescope Onesteel	Orica Rio Tinto			
Building materials Boral CSR Rinker				
Average	7.8	4.6	0.7	13.1

☐ Key drivers

Source: Granular growth decomposition database

and any net gain was insignificant for everyone except ANZ, which managed to gain just over 1 percentage point of share over 4 years (Figure 1.7).

Revenue growth was only one among several factors that have made this a highly attractive industry for the past decade. Customer inertia and stickiness, high barriers to entry (namely the need to set up distribution networks), and the four pillars policy[4] all meant that competition was based on promises of customer service rather than aggressive pricing. In 1996, the market capitalization of the big four banks plus St George was A$61 billion; by 2005, it had reached A$208 billion. Their TRS for the period was 18.9 percent,

1.7 Market-share changes among Australian banks

Indexed to 2002 market share = 100

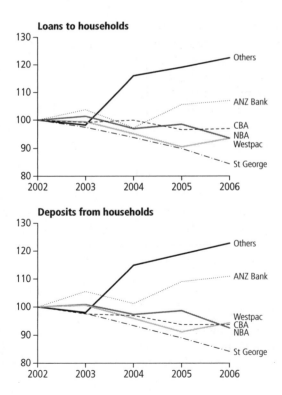

Source: Australian Prudential Regulation Authority

compared to the All Ordinaries index of 12.1 percent. The banks were definitely in the money.

Like retail banking, the insurance sector has enjoyed a strong tailwind in recent years. It has also seen a high rate of consolidation, driven by QBE, IAG, Suncorp, and Promina. In October 2006, Suncorp and Promina announced their intention to merge, creating a company with A$1.4 billion[5] in net profit. Again, market-share gains over the period had a relatively small impact in comparison to market growth and M&A. Indeed, achieving revenue growth through market-share gain can be a dangerous path in insurance, especially for the so-called "long-tail" businesses where the underwriting cost of premiums written today can't be known for some years to come.

The detail of retail

Retail is a sector in which portfolio momentum, M&A, and market-share changes have all played important roles in growth.

While Coles Myer managed to grow almost entirely on the back of market growth, making no net acquisitions during this period, it was substantially outgrown by Woolworths, Wesfarmers, and Harvey Norman, each of which gained market share *and* made acquisitions.[6] Much of the dynamic in retail in Australia over the past ten years has derived from the extension of the major supermarket chains into new categories such as fresh fruit, meat and bread, health and beauty, liquor, and fuel retailing. Woolworths has tended to move more aggressively and more effectively into each of these categories, although it has not necessarily been the first to do so.

At the same time, Woolworths made a huge investment in building a supply chain that could execute a granular strategy at scale, upgrading IT systems in its stores and distribution centres to improve the forecasting of replenishment demands. In addition, it gave back a portion of its cost savings in the form of lower consumer prices, and has gradually gained share in many of its categories.

Catching a tailwind

Some of the growth giants reshaped their portfolios in higher-growth, more attractive markets through a combination of M&A and share gain.

In 1999, Wesfarmers was a business with A$3 billion in revenue, about a third from home improvement retailing and the remainder from insurance, coal, and chemicals and fertilizers. By 2006, its revenues had reached

A\$8.9 billion, a CAGR of 16.9 percent. About half of this growth was inorganic, from acquisitions in home improvement, industrial safety, and insurance, net of almost A\$1 billion in divestments. The organic remaining half of the growth was mostly attributable to the strong tailwinds behind the coal and home improvement businesses.

The company also shifted its portfolio over the period to take advantage of the fast-growing, profitable home improvement sector. In fact, the growth of this business accounted for A\$3.2 billion of Wesfarmers' A\$5.9 billion in revenue growth over the period 1999 to 2006. Portfolio momentum growth in home improvement was a healthy 5 percent per year, contributing A\$1 billion of the \$3.2 billion growth in home improvement. A further \$1.7 billion in revenue was acquired through the purchase of Howard Smith, which added BBC Hardware, Hardware House, and Benchmark to Wesfarmers' home improvement portfolio. Finally, Wesfarmers invested heavily in marketing to create the national Bunnings brand and was rewarded with market share gains worth A\$500 million.

As we write, Wesfarmers has made a bid for the Coles Group valued at around A\$17 billion (depending on its own share price). Part of Coles' appeal is its Officeworks chain, which will help Wesfarmers continue the growth it achieved with Bunnings in retailing large ranges of non-perishable goods in a big-box format targeting consumers and small businesses. Wesfarmers is also betting that it can stretch its management skills to the troubled Coles Supermarkets division.

Over the past decade, Publishing & Broadcasting Limited (PBL) has shifted from being principally a media company to being an owner and operator of casinos. The biggest step came on 18 October 2006 when it sold half of most of its media assets to a joint venture with private-equity player CVC. Subsequently it has reduced its stake to a quarter. PBL's core capabilities arguably lie not only in managing a highly regulated business (first media, then casinos) but also in recognizing undervalued assets (by predicting market growth and timing its investments accordingly). Of PBL's A\$700 million in revenue growth derived from casinos in the period 2000–06, A\$300 million was acquired, A\$300 million came from market growth, and A\$100 million came from market-share gain as Crown established itself as perhaps the premium casino destination in Australia. The company is now expanding its casino business into Russia and Macao, betting on its ability to replicate its domestic success in very different markets.

With the resource boom carrying many companies to riches, it is tempting to attribute their success to luck. Yet luck wasn't the whole story. The giant BHP Billiton made deliberate portfolio moves to ensure it was in the right set of businesses to take advantage of the boom. This meant focusing on globally traded minerals such as iron ore and coal while avoiding stranded assets and exiting structurally difficult industries such as steel production. Through a series of investment projects and acquisitions, BHP Billiton has carved out positions in key growth markets such as China, Russia, and Brazil and key supply markets such as Australia, Chile, Brazil, West Africa, and Mongolia.

Winning on the world stage

In our experience, analysts and board members often get nervous when CEOs start to look abroad. It's true that many Australian companies have got their fingers burned when expanding overseas. Telstra had an unhappy experience with Reach (a joint venture with Hong Kong telco PCCW); both Foster's and Lion Nathan withdrew from the beer game in China after seeing losses mount; NAB's Homeside acquisition in the US cost it US$1.7 billion, with further write-offs from Michigan National; and AMP's UK adventures almost sank the company. As a result, while many Australian companies are regarded as good at exporting raw materials, few are seen as successful players on the global stage.

Yet despite the bad press, there have been some genuine success stories. A few companies have taken an in-depth look at their market segments and weighed up their capabilities honestly and thoughtfully before venturing abroad. Perhaps the best-known example is Macquarie Bank, which has expanded internationally in the niche of infrastructure financing. It buys infrastructure with natural monopoly characteristics, securitizes the income streams to offer to investors, and extracts fees from the deals, as well as for performance. It owns toll roads in North America, the UK, Portugal, France, and Germany; airports in Sydney, Rome, Copenhagen, Birmingham, Brussels, and Bristol; communications networks in the UK and Australia; gas companies and distribution in the US; and ports in China. Its total overseas assets are valued at over A$28 billion.[7] By taking a granular view of its markets and building a world-class capability in buying and managing its assets, Macquarie has become one of the most successful Australian companies on the international stage.

Another example is Rinker's success in the US. The company was formed in 2003 when CSR carved out its building materials business from its sugar and wood products businesses. Since then, Rinker has grown from a US$3.7 billion business to a US$5.3 billion business with a CAGR of 13 percent. Much of this growth came from M&A: the company spent US$1.9 billion on 47 acquisitions,[8] focusing on small to medium-sized building material businesses in the south and west of the US.

Market reactions to the first few deals were negative, as witnessed by Morgan Stanley's comment in 2003: "In our view, it is difficult to have a competitive advantage for acquisitions. As long as competitive acquisition tension is present we struggle to see how acquisitions can be purchased at a price that will lead to a return above the cost of capital." But by 2007, when Rinker was acquired by Cemex for US$15.3 billion, it was clear that the strategy had worked: "[Rinker has a] proven growth strategy with the balance sheet to support it. More importantly, we view its track record since demerger in capital management as exemplary."[9]

The secret of this success was not Rinker's skill at managing building materials businesses. It was much more granular: building materials is invariably a very local business given the high costs of transportation relative to extraction, and operational and pricing discipline matter. Like CRH, the global Irish building materials giant,[10] Rinker understood how to buy and run this type of local business.

Other players that have taken a granular view have prospered outside Australia. Westfield, one of a series of globally successful Australian property players, has found a niche in the highly competitive US market in developing and managing shopping centers. Its approach to identifying the characteristics that make a center attractive is highly granular: it favors centers in major trade areas with high-quality specialty retailers and national chain stores. As one analyst explains, "They have developed an almost unique capability in constrained site development and redevelopment of existing centers, with minimal disruption to trading."[11] Westfield now operates 121 shopping centers valued at A$60 billion across Australia, New Zealand, the US, and the UK.

Another Australian company with a strong international track record is CSL. From its origins as a government department set up during World War I to guarantee Australia's supply of sera, vaccines, and other biological compounds, it has grown into a world leader in plasma therapeutics. Following public listing in 1994, it embarked on a series of astute acquisitions to build global leadership positions in a number of categories. Along with Merck, CSL was a key player in the research and development of the vaccine against HPV, one of the leading causes of cervical cancer.

What next?

Unfortunately, we can't take the events of the past as an indication of what will happen in the future. Looking at the things that made a growth giant successful over the past ten years isn't likely to shed much light on what executives should do in the next ten years. However, we can identify a few important factors that will influence the growth landscape for large companies in Australia by affecting their strategic choices, their growth opportunities, and the way they think about their future.

Don't bank on luck

It's sometimes said that it's better to be lucky than good. Over the past decade, banks had more than their fair share of luck – which is not to say that they weren't also run well. Eventually, though, luck runs out; the tailwinds that have favored your sector of the economy will shift to someone else's. And we shouldn't forget the saying that the more you practise, the luckier you get. Those that have benefited from tailwinds through deliberate moves need to keep making their own luck, and those that just happened to be in the right place at the right time had better head for the practice range!

Most people recognize that the home loan market – although still booming in Western Australia and Queensland – has started to slow. So the big banks are fighting for small to medium-sized business customers and starting to price more aggressively to win share in transaction accounts and credit cards. They must find a way to continue to deliver the growth that is built into their stock prices in the absence of the double-digit market growth that has carried them for the past ten years. For some, this requires looking outside Australia, as we see below. At the same time, the strong growth of the Australian industry, a stable geopolitical environment, and Australia's proximity to Asia have all served to attract overseas interest which will intensify the challenge to hold on to market share. HBOS, Rabobank, Citibank, and GE Capital all have serious positions here.

Delivering growth in these circumstances demands not only a strategy that can keep the bank's market position in line with the shifts in pockets of growth, but also excellent execution capable of minimizing share losses. While market-share gains are unlikely to make many Australian companies into growth giants, this is not an area they can afford to neglect. Unless commercial capabilities such as pricing, marketing-spend effectiveness, and salesforce effectiveness are relentlessly improved, leakages in margin and share will force CEOs to take growth off the agenda and focus on performance.

Local M&A gets tougher

The waves of consolidation over the past 15 years have left most Australian industries dominated by a few large national players. We have two beer companies that together command more than 85 percent of the market, not to mention two pay-TV companies with more than 80 percent, two supermarkets with over 70 percent, three petroleum-refining companies with almost 90 percent, three ceramic-tile and pipe manufacturing companies with more than 70 percent, and four banks with more than 80 percent of their respective sectors.[12] Steel has gone from three players to two, with OneSteel and Bluescope carving up Smorgon. Even expansion across the Tasman into New Zealand is getting tougher. Since ANZ's purchase of the National Bank of New Zealand in 2003, each of the top four banks in New Zealand has been owned by one of its counterparts in Australia. Woolworths has bought Foodland Group in New Zealand and invested in the Warehouse Group with a decision pending from the NZ Commerce Commission on whether it can move to full ownership. For many of these industries there is no room for further consolidation, as any further moves would be likely to infringe competition regulations.

Even so, some industries still have a way to go before there is full consolidation. Look at the frenetic activity in the energy sector as Alinta, AGL, and Origin jostle to shape their portfolios and determine who will consolidate or be consolidated. Origin has placed a big bet on upstream gas, integrating downstream to sell the gas either as molecules or converted into electrons. AGL has aggressively consolidated the retail market with its Alinta deal and the acquisition of Powerdirect from the Queensland government. It is also integrating back upstream to secure generation assets, and had concluded a number of big deals before the recent (and predicted) spike in wholesale electricity prices. Meanwhile, both AGL and Origin have divested their infrastructure businesses, shifting their portfolios towards the higher-growth retail and generation markets. The potential privatization of the entire NSW energy sector and Queensland generation assets will determine the next wave of growth.

Faced with fewer M&A opportunities in their existing businesses, companies will be pushed to larger and perhaps riskier deals outside their traditional domains. Foster's is still under pressure from analysts to produce returns from its A$7.8 billion of assets in wine.[13] CCA acquired SPC Ardmona, betting on its distribution system to boost canned fruit and juice sales. It is also moving into liquor with a distribution agreement with Maxxium and has announced its intention to enter the highly profitable but slow-growing beer market. Wesfarmers is looking at parts of Coles, betting that its retail skills in home improvement and hardware can be extended to office supplies. The banks have faced heavy criticism for their forays into wealth management, although we believe these will be viewed favorably in time.

With growth at a premium and most sectors highly consolidated, those deals that do become available will be heavily contested by both corporations and private equity.

The private-equity way to go

A co-founder of one of the world's top private-equity firms recently remarked that the whole of Australia seemed to be up for sale. A wall of liquidity has hit the market, fuelled by local liquidity from the country's compulsory superannuation contribution scheme[14] as well as its emergence on the radar of global firms that view it as an attractive market with ripe and highly concentrated industry structures. Private-equity deals were worth US$15 billion in 2006, up from US$650 million in 2000, and represented 16 percent of all deals. Given that private equity constituted 30 percent of all deals in the US in 2006, this leaves plenty of room for growth.[15] Despite the collapse of some high-profile deals including Coles Group, Qantas, and Flight Centre, not to mention a tightening of global credit triggered by the collapse of the US sub-prime mortgage market, private equity will continue to be an important player in the Australian corporate landscape in the coming years.

Its presence will have three main effects on Australian companies. First, it will force a reassessment of portfolios at a granular level, either voluntarily or in response to an unsolicited bid. Companies will need to focus on extracting performance improvements from their businesses, but not at the expense of neglecting the fundamental strategic question about which businesses to continue to own. If they aren't the natural owners of the businesses they are in, they are unlikely to find a better time to sell.

Second, the price of M&A deals will go up. Private equity is backing its governance model and outbidding strategic buyers in many markets; Australia is no exception.

Third, assets will come back onto the market as the private-equity cycle runs its course and sponsors look to exit, releasing another round of M&A opportunities to strategic buyers.

International expansion is back

The high concentration of many of Australia's industries means that companies confined to the domestic market will hit the limits of growth unless their sector has the good fortune to be enjoying a particularly strong tailwind. So should they, like some of our growth giants, be looking to international markets for growth?

At present, only 13 of Australia's top 50 companies by value get more than half their revenue from outside Australia and New Zealand, and there are 16 that get 1 percent or less (Figure 1.8.) Given these low levels of international investment and the constraints on growth at home, more Australian companies are starting to make offshore forays. Among banks, for example, Westpac[16] is the only one not to have made acquisition moves in Asia. NAB has moved into Hong Kong, Japan, and Singapore; ANZ into Indonesia, China, Cambodia, and Vietnam; CBA into China, India, and Indonesia. So far, their international businesses are still relatively small: just 7 percent of revenues for ANZ and 6 percent for CBA. NAB leads the pack with more than 20 percent of its revenues deriving from overseas, mostly from Europe. Other sectors are also experiencing a revival in international expansion: Harvey Norman is entering India, PBL is investing in casinos in Macau and Russia, and Toll has acquired SembCorp Logistics in Singapore.

Analyst and board sentiment seems to have shifted. Extreme caution about overseas moves has given way to a readiness to challenge CEOs to articulate their international aspirations. The key issue is what insight companies have into where to play: can they pick the attractive spaces and do they know how to win? Granularity is central to ensure the insight is real and the market and business models adequately understood. One rule of thumb is to keep pushing for a more granular definition of the market that is being entered until the projected revenue accounts for at least 20 to 30 percent of it. This way, companies avoid the false confidence of believing a small share of a big market is achievable.

Granularity is also vital for Australia's global aspirants. Most Australian companies have no chance of competing for the big deals against global players with balance sheets ten times the size of their own, so they need to

1.8 Global or regional champions?

Share of revenue derived outside Australia and New Zealand for ASX top 50*

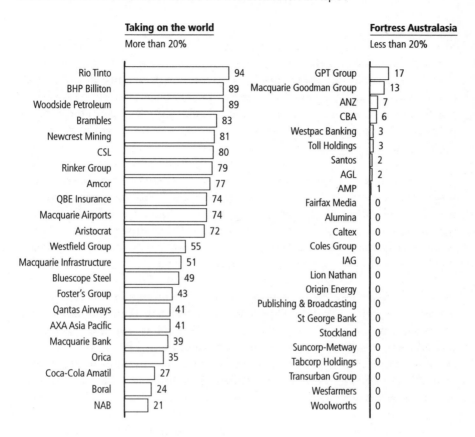

Taking on the world More than 20%		Fortress Australasia Less than 20%	
Rio Tinto	94	GPT Group	17
BHP Billiton	89	Macquarie Goodman Group	13
Woodside Petroleum	89	ANZ	7
Brambles	83	CBA	6
Newcrest Mining	81	Westpac Banking	3
CSL	80	Toll Holdings	3
Rinker Group	79	Santos	2
Amcor	77	AGL	2
QBE Insurance	74	AMP	1
Macquarie Airports	74	Fairfax Media	0
Aristocrat	72	Alumina	0
Westfield Group	55	Caltex	0
Macquarie Infrastructure	51	Coles Group	0
Bluescope Steel	49	IAG	0
Foster's Group	43	Lion Nathan	0
Qantas Airways	41	Origin Energy	0
AXA Asia Pacific	41	Publishing & Broadcasting	0
Macquarie Bank	39	St George Bank	0
Orica	35	Stockland	0
Coca-Cola Amatil	27	Suncorp-Metway	0
Boral	24	Tabcorp Holdings	0
NAB	21	Transurban Group	0
		Wesfarmers	0
		Woolworths	0

* Excluding Centro Properties, Lend Lease, Telstra, and DB RReef Trust, where there was insufficient information
  on geographic segments
Source: Annual reports; McKinsey analysis

be able to find the deals that never make it onto the radar screens of these behemoths.

Where the choices lie

After a period of extensive change, companies sometimes allow themselves to be taken over by an execution mindset, while strategy takes a back seat. To some extent they are right: they will have to raise the bar on execution if they are to hold on to market share and maintain profitability. Foreign entrants, private equity, and shifting tailwinds will punish those that don't improve their competitiveness as quickly as their competitors do. This may seem obvious, but we often see business plans to grow market share through a series of initiatives that assume the competition is standing still.

More ambitious companies may have articulated bold growth aspirations, but without knowing where the growth will come from. The imperative for them is to convert the aspirations into a compelling growth direction and granular strategies. They need to start by taking a dispassionate view of their portfolio of businesses at a granular level and checking whether their business plans clearly articulate the "where to compete" choices that will deliver their growth, both domestically and internationally.

Companies face a genuine choice: should they pursue profitable growth or maximize value in a low-growth future? Instead of being stuck in the middle, some may do better to take growth off the agenda, drive performance, and return money to shareholders. Time is another factor in the mix. While CEOs often work to a short-term agenda, boards may want to ensure that companies take a longer-term perspective.

To be sure, we believe there are some Australian companies for which growth is the wrong choice. These are the companies that have limited opportunities to consolidate their markets or leverage their capabilities in new spaces, and few international markets where they can win. Equally, there are Australian companies that have argued themselves into a low-growth future when they should be redefining the boundaries of their industries, thinking creatively about their capabilities, and developing granular insight into the world outside their shores.

■ ■ ■

So who will be Australia's growth giants ten years from now? If history is any guide, we can expect that a fair number of today's growth giants will still be on the list. But there will also be a new generation of companies that find growth within Australia and internationally and are rewarded by the market. Either way, the companies that make it onto the list will be the ones that have worked out how to create their own luck by making perceptive granular choices about where to compete.

NOTES

1   Global Insight, Real GDP 1989–2005 (base year 2000).

2   Over the fifteen-year period 1991–2005.

3   See chapter 2 of *The Granularity of Growth*.

4   Established by the Australian federal government to be administered by APRA (Australian Prudential Regulation Authority) and ACCC (Australian Competition and Consumer Commission), the policy prohibits Australia's four largest banks (National Australia Bank, Commonwealth Bank of Australia, Westpac Bank, and Australia and New Zealand Bank) from merging with one another, the intention being to prevent the banking industry from becoming a duopoly or even a monopoly in which one or two banks could set high fees for transactions and other banking services.

5   For the year ending June 2006, from Promina's Scheme booklet.

6   Admittedly, share gains are likely to be overestimated at this level of aggregation because some gains from portfolio momentum will look like gains in share. Take a company that sells plasma-screen TVs and washing machines. If we take the market for appliances as a whole, it may appear to be gaining share. But if we dig down deeper, we may find that it has focused more on the fast-growing plasma-screen TV market and less on the quieter washing-machine market: in effect, it has made better market choices at a granular level to capitalize on portfolio momentum.

7   Thompsons company profile.

8   Between 1998 and July 2006, JP Morgan analyst report, 10 July 2006.

9   JP Morgan analyst report, 10 July 2006.

10 Described in chapter 6 of *The Granularity of Growth*.

11 UBS Investment Research, Westfield, 6 July 2004.

12 IBIS reports on market share.

13 Fosters Group 2005 annual report (year ending 30 June 2006).

14 Australian employers are required to make superannuation contributions of 9 percent on behalf of their employees. After more than a decade of compulsory contributions, these funds now amount to over A$1 trillion, leaving Australia with the world's highest per capita investment in managed funds.

15 AVCJ, Capital IQ, Dealogic.

16 Westpac has grown organically in Asia by setting up offices in Singapore, Beijing, Hong Kong, and Jakarta.

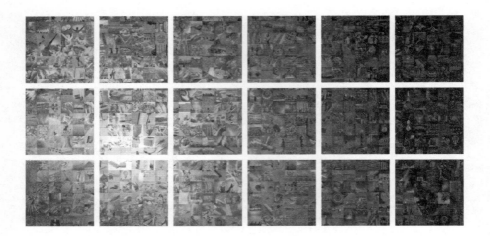

2

China's gigantic growth

Gordon Orr

YOU MIGHT BE FORGIVEN for wondering why we need a chapter on China at all. Its exceptional growth is hardly news. What more is there to say about an economy that has grown at over 10 percent a year for 25 years, rising from eighth to fourth largest in the world?[1] Growth, it would seem, is everywhere, and it has made China the single largest geographic market for many consumer and industrial products.

Take mobile phones: sales grew from 25 to 131 million a year between 1999 and 2006, making China the world's biggest market.[2] Or take refrigerators, up from 9.5 million to 12.5 million sales a year, an increase of 31 percent in seven years.[3] Or take electricity, where China's new generating capacity of 385.5 gigawatts[4] equates to five times the total capacity of the United Kingdom.[5] Or take steel, where the 421.5 million tons produced in 2006 represents more than a third of the world total.[6]

Yet this seemingly simple story conceals a more complex reality. First of all, growth may be ubiquitous, but it is unevenly distributed – by sector, by geography, and by market positioning. Some sectors stayed small for a long time before growing; some have stayed small for multinationals; and some are still small for everyone. Computer software and IT services are among the sectors that are only now starting to become a scale industry in China. The leading Chinese IT services provider still generates revenues of less than US$100 million, a fraction of the revenues of the leading US and Indian providers.

Second, companies that enter a particular sector at much the same time can face very different outcomes in terms of their market share and the revenue they achieve. How did SAB Miller become the largest brewer in China while Foster's and several others chose to exit? What allowed Yum Brands, with its Kentucky Fried Chicken and Pizza Hut restaurants, to generate more than US$200 million in profit here in 2006, while Burger King is only opening its first few stores in 2007? And what is it about this market that has enabled General Motors to sell more Buicks than it does in the US and take pole position ahead of Toyota?

Below, we look at how companies' strategies have shaped their growth in China and consider the factors that have contributed to their success. We explore what makes this market unique and examine the constraints that local and multinational companies have had to overcome to achieve sustained growth. We also offer a few predictions of what will shape growth in China in the coming decade.

A complex picture

Beneath the surface, China's growth looks much more patchy, both within industries and across different geographical regions. A sector may grow very slowly for many years, suddenly reach a tipping point, grow at more than 50 percent a year for several years, reach an interim maturity of much slower growth, and then experience a new surge in growth. The car industry is currently experiencing its first big surge (Figure 2.1). Another example is the software sector, which grew very slowly for many years but has leaped forward in the past three years with a growth rate close to 50 percent, as legitimate software became more widely accepted. By contrast, few service businesses are close to the tipping point even today.

These sudden growth spurts present a challenge even for the strongest businesses. If you aren't ready to grow with or ahead of the market during periods of hyper-growth, you will quickly fall from a market leader to a follower, or from a follower to a marginal player. Preparing for the tipping point and being quick to spot it when it comes are critical for any company wanting to take advantage of market growth in China.

Similarly, growth is "lumpy" across China's regions. For many years, it was focused on and around a few top-tier cities, but this is changing. China is

2.1 China's booming car market*

Unit sales volume, thousands

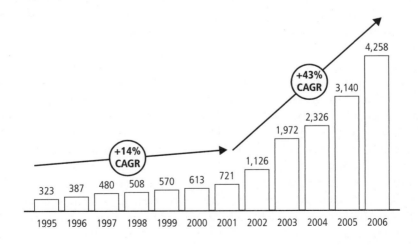

323 387 480 508 570 613 721 1,126 1,972 2,326 3,140 4,258

+14% CAGR   +43% CAGR

1995 1996 1997 1998 1999 2000 2001 2002 2003 2004 2005 2006

* For locally-made passenger cars
Source: CAIN

undergoing a demographic shift: the vast majority of those now entering the middle class for the first time come from second- and third-tier cities. The effect can be seen in patterns of demand: customers from these cities now account for more than 80 percent of mobile phone sales, for instance.[7]

Businesses need to take heed of these changes: timing is all. If a company enters the lower-tier cities too early, there will be no market for its products. Consider Fuji Xerox, which pushed its copiers widely in the mid-market during the 1990s, only to have to pull back and consolidate. On the other hand, entering too late will mean that the company misses the opportunity to shape the market. LG Electronics is playing catch-up in white goods in China, having confined itself to the top-tier market in its early years here.

Another contributor to China's patchy growth is its massive investment in infrastructure, which has driven over 45 percent of GDP growth in the past four years.[8] Much of this investment has gone into building apartments, constructed at staggering rates as high as 2,643 million square meters a year.[9] Each new housing project leads to a burst of consumer expenditure, much of it outside the high-profile centers of Beijing, Shanghai, and Shenzhen, which jointly account for less than 15 percent of all consumer spending.

Other investment has gone into transport infrastructure. The city of Mianyang used to be more than six hours' drive from Chengdu by two-lane road; it is now within two hours' reach by express highway. Local businesses such as Changhong previously had to rely on an unreliable rail link to ship all their goods; now they can use road transport to reach a broader range of customers.

The geographic lumpiness of growth is easily explained: China is a continent-sized market. Strength in one region does not automatically lead to success nationwide, the lack of adequate road infrastructure has been an obstacle, and consumer tastes differ widely from region to region. You may have great insight into the consumer in Shanghai, but it won't be much help to you in Dalian or Kunming. This phenomenon is by no means unique to China: consider how regional the US remained up to about 30 years ago, before the days of Wal-Mart and Best Buy. But things are starting to change: the success of Procter & Gamble and Mengniu shows that it is now practical to serve customers on a nationwide basis. Started up in 1999, Mengniu has captured over 30 percent of China's milk market and achieved revenue in excess of US$2 billion in 2006.[10]

Constraints on business growth still exist, however. Opportunities for large-scale M&A are very limited, and some sectors, largely those dominated by state-owned enterprises, are off limits to non-Chinese businesses. They include armament, power generation and distribution, oil and petrochemicals, telecommunications, coal, aviation, and shipping. Some restrictions affect Chinese companies as well as multinationals, preventing even the largest local companies from making acquisitions and consolidating their sectors.

There are several reasons why this state of affairs has persisted: local government resistance, conflicting interests in the central ministries, the lack of a framework for valuing acquisitions, and inexperience in completing mergers. Only in sectors that are predominantly private – consumer electronics, PCs, the internet, new retail sectors – have acquisitions been allowed. However, some of these barriers will be overcome, especially by locals. Domestic M&A in the first half of 2007 rose to US$55 billion: still small by US standards, but a hefty 40 percent increase on the previous year.[11]

Though a company's relations with government are often important, strong relationships in one city or province are unlikely to help it achieve national reach, as local influence does not necessarily extend further afield. Government bodies do however play a broader role in shaping market opportunities and controlling the evolution of the regulatory framework. In financial services, for instance, regulation has slowly evolved to the point where it now provides for the creation of financial service holding companies. In telecom services, the finalization of 3G licenses seems imminent after years of waiting.

Often, though, the government's most important role is that of customer (or owner of the customer). In sectors as varied as power, telecom, airlines, and banking, the government holds majority stakes in all the large players. As a result, it dominates purchase decisions, which can often be influenced by local concerns and interests. This is one reason why the multinationals that are successful in China tend to have very strong government relations teams. At GE and Siemens, for example, such teams are charged with building long-term relationships at multiple levels of central and local government. GE's investment in mass advertising and its sponsorship of the Beijing Olympics are aspects of this strategy.

A final factor shaping the pattern of growth in China is the high savings rate. Chinese consumers put away a quarter of their annual income on average.[12] Some of these savings are made in anticipation of a major purchase such as a house, a car, or a child's education. However, a large portion is prompted by the need to save for future healthcare needs and old age, since expectations that the government will provide social security are limited. The creation of higher-quality personal savings schemes and insurance policies for the emerging middle class is likely to free up some of this capital, as it has done in other Asian countries.

Sources of growth

To understand where China's growth is coming from, we can break it down into the three components of portfolio momentum, M&A, and market-share growth. It quickly becomes apparent that there are significant differences between China and the rest of the world. The most obvious are the limited role that M&A has played in the economy and the periods of hyper-growth that many markets have experienced.[13]

Portfolio momentum

Being in the right market and poised to grow once a sector reaches an inflection point and spurts into explosive growth has been key for the success of many businesses in China. This is a market where growing at 10 or 20 percent doesn't guarantee a leadership position. What really matters is the ability to capture the three or four years of 40 to 50 percent growth generated by a growth spurt.

Even early movers can find long-standing leadership positions eroded if they don't move quickly, as Volkswagen found to its cost. When demand for entry-level sedan cars went through the roof, it didn't have the products, channels, or brand position it needed to succeed. By contrast, Lenovo's thorough organizational discipline meant it was ready when the PC market took off and was able to make the transition from one of the pack to industry champion with a market share of 28 percent.[14] Even so, diversification into other product areas in pursuit of the next wave of growth has proven as challenging for Lenovo as it has for many others. Its only large-scale success here has been in handsets.

Haier is another company that was well prepared for hyper-growth. When the first wave of home ownership struck, it was ready with a product and a service network that could take advantage of low labor costs. As a result, it was able to achieve a 24 percent market share in white goods within three or four years.[15]

M&A

Unlike in many other markets in Asia and further afield, inorganic growth has so far been of limited importance in China. The legacy of protected local champions remains strong, preventing consolidation even in sectors that clearly need it, such as steel, and even when consolidation is directed by a government ministry, as with Baosteel's acquisition of 69.6 percent of the Bayi I&S Group. Lack of experience in managing deals and management intransigence can stop the benefits of integration being realized or even stall a deal altogether. Yet despite this, many Chinese companies are seeking to grow through acquisitions, having struggled to grow organically. As we see later, this lack of experience of domestic acquisition creates significant barriers to international growth.

Partly as a result, partnerships with local enterprises were the most common entry vehicle for multinationals until 2001,[16] largely because of government regulations precluding outright acquisition or organic investment. The pendulum has gradually started to swing the other way as more and more sectors have been opened up to direct international investment, largely because of China's accession to the World Trade Organization (Figure 2.2). Even today, though, Chinese law requires that foreign investment be made through joint ventures in certain sectors such as the automotive industry. The government also has a list of strategic sectors (including steel, non-ferrous metals, and machine tools) where foreign takeovers are not yet allowed.

2.2 Foreign direct investment in China

US$ billions; percent

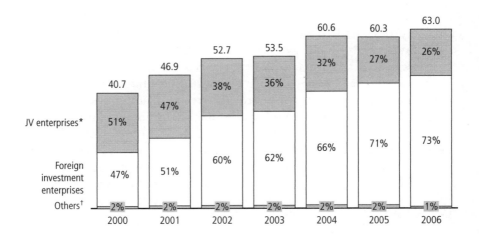

* Including joint venture enterprises and cooperative operation enterprises
† Including foreign investment share enterprises, cooperative development, and others
Source: *China Statistical Yearbook 2007*

There are relatively few cases where a multinational has acquired or invested in a Chinese enterprise because of its inherent strength. In brewing, Budweiser invested in Tsingtao while SAB invested in Snowflake, among others. In beverages, Danone invested in two of China's leading bottled-water companies – buying Nowada outright and acquiring 51 percent of Wahaha – to form the foundation of its Chinese beverage business in the late 1990s.

Market share

Growth in market share is the norm for a successful business in China. It may result from an early move into a new region where the market is opening up, or entry at a new price point, or entry through a new channel that is just coming into use. An example of the latter is Nokia's move from national distributors to local distributors and direct delivery. It enabled the company to get ahead of the pack by achieving greater control over its distribution and ensured it was fully prepared for the emergence of the consumer electronics superstores that have reshaped the market in the past few years. Procter & Gamble, Mars, and Coca-Cola have all led the way in extending coverage deep into the provinces, to fifth-tier cities and beyond.

A final element that determines whether companies are successful in gaining share is having the organizational discipline to execute well in times of rapid growth. This involves being able to recruit rapidly, having systems in place to identify where the hot spots are, and being able to scale up distribution and service channels in a controlled fashion.

Chinese market leaders such as Ping An, Lenovo, and Haier all developed these abilities early on. Ping An set up a world-class development facility in Shenzhen to help it train and deploy the tens of thousands of insurance agents it recruits each year. Lenovo's supply chain incorporates a tight feedback loop with local distributors that provides it with daily information on its own and competitors' sales, enabling it to adjust its inventories to take account of likely demand. Haier was able to develop distinctiveness and cultivate a caring image for its brand by expanding its service team to respond to customer complaints. It is able to reach the home of any customer in the hundreds of cities where it operates within 24 hours of a complaint being made.

Who grew?

In several sectors, national champions virtually have first rights over growth opportunities. Owned by the government through the State-Owned Asset Supervision and Administration Commission (SASAC), they formally hold regional or national monopolies in telecommunications, energy, and industrial sectors. Financial services enterprises report separately to the China Banking Regulatory Commission (CBRC). China Mobile has used its incumbent leadership position to acquire over 300 million customers[17] and achieve a market capitalization of US$217 billion,[18] far outstripping attacker China Unicom.

In sectors that have emerged more recently (largely those that sell direct to consumers), it's often private Chinese companies and not multinationals that are the winners (Figure 2.3). Li Ning, for instance, has succeeded in sports apparel and Bosideng in fur clothing.

2.3 Market share in consumer sectors
Percent, 2006

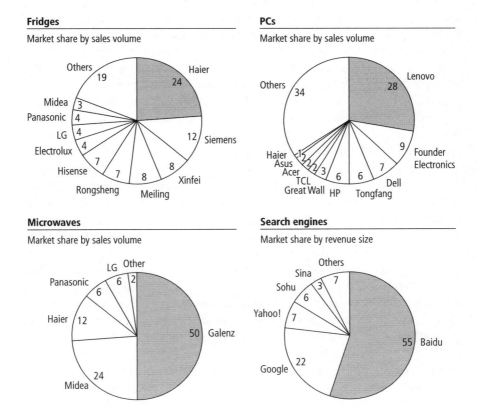

Fridges
Market share by sales volume

PCs
Market share by sales volume

Microwaves
Market share by sales volume

Search engines
Market share by revenue size

Source: Sino-MR; iResearch; Gartner

A similar pattern can be seen in other sectors too. Nine Dragons Paper Company has created a pre-eminent position in paper recycling, having established a business worth US$10.2 billion within five years of starting up. SunTech has become one of the world's largest solar panel producers with a market value of over US$5 billion by leveraging low research and production costs to produce a thriving domestic business supplying low-cost equipment.

Venturing abroad

Chinese companies are now beginning to look overseas for their growth. Their relative inexperience in operating internationally means they face many risks. Yet turning to foreign markets is a natural if not vital step for market leaders accustomed to growth rates of 30 percent or more, especially when their market share prevents them from growing faster than their market.

The Chinese companies that venture overseas tend to follow the path of least resistance and grow organically, first building sales in markets such as Russia, Southeast Asia, and Latin America before expanding into the tougher markets of North America and Europe. Telecom equipment supplier Huawei experienced its first successful wave of international expansion in Latin America and the former Soviet Union. In parallel, it attempted to build sales in the US, but a combination of legal challenges over intellectual property, high management turnover, and the lack of a local service organization meant that it met only limited success. By 2006, though, Huawei had achieved international orders worth more than US$8.5 billion and is rapidly becoming a strong contender in the top tier of its sector globally. Another Chinese company with a strong international presence is automobile manufacturer Chery, which has six overseas assembly plants in five countries with sales of over 50,000 units.

The extent of Chinese companies' international ventures shouldn't be over-estimated, however. Even now, only half of the 57 largest technology, media, and telecom players have any international activities at all, for instance. In other sectors, the proportion of market leaders active overseas is lower still: for instance, in the consumer, energy, materials, and finance sectors it ranges from 40 to as little as 25 percent (Figure 2.4).

At the other extreme, Chinese enterprises are raising their profile in sectors such as PCs and consumer electronics, where companies including Lenovo and TCL are establishing a presence and making direct investments in international markets. Chinese consumer electronics used to be sold through distribution agents in overseas markets, masking their origins. Leading TV

2.4 How international are China's big companies?

Share of top 500 companies by revenue with international activities,* percent

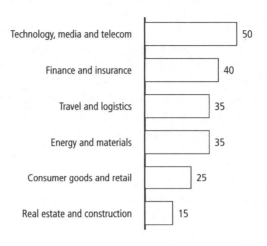

Technology, media and telecom	50
Finance and insurance	40
Travel and logistics	35
Energy and materials	35
Consumer goods and retail	25
Real estate and construction	15

* Includes global export, investment, sales, and R&D activity for the period 2005 to April 2007

manufacturers Changhong and SVA both built large US businesses in this way. However, the model fell out of favor after Changhong's public dispute with its distributor over US$500 million of receivables due. As Wal-Mart, Best Buy, and others built up their sourcing operations in China, manufacturers had less need to use agents.

Another change came in 2004–05, when Lenovo and TCL both bought leading international companies and their brands. Not only were their purchases much larger than their domestic businesses, but they dramatically raised the profile of Chinese foreign direct investment. This trend has continued. In 2006, direct investment from China reached over US$16 billion, up from only US$3 billion three years earlier.[19] Much of this investment is in the basic materials sector, made with the aim of controlling the supply of industrial raw materials, but an increasing amount goes to the high-tech and automotive sectors.

The broadening of Chinese companies' investment portfolios reflects their widening aspirations. Their investment strategy has progressed from the acquisition of raw materials to the acquisition of intellectual property, brands, and access to large-scale markets. For instance, Shanghai and Nanjing

Automotive have recently acquired intellectual property in the UK (from the remains of Rover) and Korea. Similarly, Chinese machine-tool companies such as Shenyang Machine have acquired German enterprises for their intellectual property assets.

The desire of Chinese high-tech and consumer electronics companies to secure rapid access to new markets for their products has given further impetus to overseas investments. Organic investment has often proved painfully slow and many companies have stumbled through lack of international brand recognition and experience in meeting the needs of overseas consumers and managing overseas executives.

At the moment, one factor above all is driving China's foreign acquisitions: the desire to gain access to internationally experienced management teams to help lead the further development of their global businesses. Many enterprises with aspirations overseas have little international experience in their top teams. TCL had almost none when it acquired Thomson's TV business; at Lenovo, meanwhile, only the CFO had substantial international experience. These companies' leaders recognize that their senior management, while successful and talented, have gained their experience largely or entirely in China. Inevitably, it will take time for them to grow into their new global role. Bringing management in from the outside can help speed up the process.

2.5 Struggling to realize the value from M&A
Returns two years after a major international acquisition, January 2002–05

	Number of deals*	2-year normalized TRS[†] Percent
China	38	−3
Hong Kong	101	7
India	159	11
South Korea	60	6

* Only public acquirers with 2 years of TRS data with M&A between January 2000 and January 2005 included
[†] Total shareholder returns, a measure of total stock return including dividends. Normalized TRS is a measure of excess return over the stock market in which the stock is listed
Source: Datastream; Dealogic; BSE; KOSPI; SSE; HKSE

International M&A presents Chinese companies with specific challenges. One is that it puts them in the public eye and exposes their every step to close scrutiny. Press interest in CNOOC's bid for Unocal and Haier's bid for Maytag meant there was no time for the internal consensus building that is an essential part of much Chinese decision making. Instead, external stakeholders such as politicians, unions, and journalists ended up shaping the process. By contrast, the fact that Lenovo's acquisition of IBM's PC business was confidential until the deal was announced made a major contribution to its success.

International M&A is not yet a proven path for Chinese companies. For most recent acquisitions the jury is still out, if only because not enough time has elapsed since the deals were done. So far the signs are mixed: in aggregate, the returns in share price for international acquirers relative to local market indices have lagged those of counterparts in Hong Kong, South Korea, and India (Figure 2.5).

Having conducted an in-depth analysis of more than 20 early movers, we have identified several success factors for would-be Chinese acquirers to note:

Ensure that your strategic rationale is clear and that your top team is behind it. Before making an international move, Lenovo's leadership spent months in establishing a common understanding among the top team of the lack of sustainability of a go-it-alone approach in China and the consequent need for greater global scale.

Make sure you have a solid understanding of the value of the target and its downside as well as its upside. Chinese acquirers are sometimes surprised to find out how much effort it takes to turn around an acquisition target, as when TCL bought Thomson. The scale of the payments that need to be made for services such as IT and HR, and even for developing the sales channel, can surprise even the largest of companies.

Evaluate the target management team. Because of their limited international experience, Chinese executives find it hard to assess how far the incumbent management bears responsibility for a target's underperformance.

Create a coherent culture and widely understood management model that works globally and isn't simply an extension of the informal and implicit processes that have evolved over time in your domestic operations. Merely getting used to management meetings involving people on the other side of the world can require a major cultural change in some companies.

What's next?

We can expect the rapid growth of the Chinese economy to continue. Many sectors including IT services, international travel, and tourism will experience new market inflection points with spurts of hyper-growth that create opportunities for nimble companies to leap ahead of the pack.

China's increasing capabilities will also provide new foundations for growth. The country's universities are creating nodes of innovation in areas such as nanotechnology, aspects of biotechnology, and solar-cell development that are likely to facilitate new growth opportunities. Many high-tech multi-nationals including Intel and Microsoft are already using Chinese skills, and as protection for intellectual property rights improves, more and more enterprises are likely to set up R&D centers here.

The increasing sophistication of Chinese customers opens up further growth opportunities. As they evolve from first-time buyers into repeat customers, their experience and insight into what they want from a product grow and

2.6 Ownership at the market segment level

Percent

□ Chinese   ■ Foreign

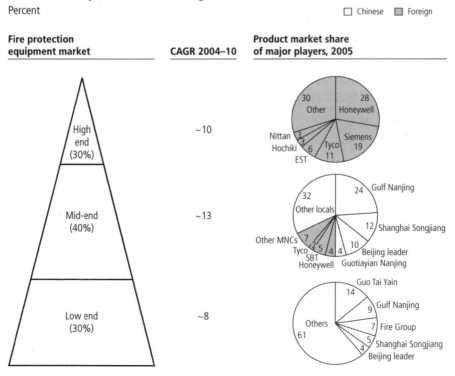

Fire protection equipment market	CAGR 2004–10	Product market share of major players, 2005

their needs and expectations accordingly become more elaborate. In response, Chinese companies must become more adept at segmenting their markets and tailoring their messages, products, and channels in response to the needs of their increasingly demanding customers.

For all their great growth, Chinese markets will become more challenging. As mid-sized Chinese enterprises become stronger and more capable, competition is likely to increase. Only five years ago, many multinationals faced hardly any local competition in high-end or even mid-range segments of the market (unlike low-end markets, where they already had difficulty competing with local companies on price). Competition from Chinese companies is now on the increase in some mid- and higher-end segments, such as the fire protection equipment market (Figure 2.6).

■ ■ ■

In future, growing as fast as the market – rapid though that growth may be – will be a ticket to play, not a winning hand. What will separate the growth giants from the unrewarded will be the ability to grow *faster* than the market during its growth spurts. Though M&A is likely to remain restricted within China, it may well become the favored path for local players seeking international expansion.

NOTES

[1] Ranking in terms of total GDP for the years 1981 and 2006 (IMF).
[2] CCID, Sino-MR, DB, Gartner, Norson.
[3] Euromonitor.
[4] China Electricity Council.
[5] UK Department of Trade and Industry, *Meeting the Energy Challenge 2007.*
[6] International Iron and Steel Institution.
[7] Sino-MR.
[8] *China Statistical Yearbook 2006.*
[9] *Ibid.*
[10] Mengniu annual report, A. C. Nielsen.
[11] Dealogic.
[12] McKinsey personal financial services survey, 2004.
[13] We are not focusing here on the export growth that is based on manufacturing or sourcing in China and then shipping abroad.
[14] Sino-MR, iResearch, Gartner.
[15] *Ibid.*
[16] *China Statistical Yearbook 2006.*
[17] Information from China Mobile's website.
[18] Hong Kong Stock Exchange, 28 June 2007.
[19] MOFCOM.

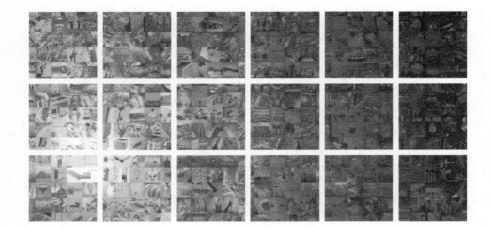

3

The Gulf Cooperation Council: Fuelled by strong growth

Herbert Pohl

THE REGION OF THE WORLD represented by the Gulf Cooperation Council (GCC) deserves much more attention from the business world than it usually gets. Bahrain, Kuwait, Oman, Qatar, Saudi Arabia, and the United Arab Emirates (UAE) have collectively shown very strong GDP growth. Although real GDP growth has been running at around 6 percent over the past five years – lower than China's or India's – it doesn't tell the whole story. If we look at *nominal* GDP growth in the region, we see a spectacular increase of 16 percent a year over the past five years.[1]

The GCC governments have made use of the current windfall to invest in projects designed to develop and diversify their economies in the long term. In addition to these projects, which are costing over a trillion dollars, they have invested in education and healthcare, and substantially reduced their external debt. Saudi Arabia's debt has fallen from a peak of 97 percent of GDP in 2002 to less than 41 percent in 2005, while Kuwait's has declined from 32 to 17 percent. This contrasts with the way the GCC countries spent their petrodollars during the last boom and will provide the region with a more solid basis for sustainable economic growth. At present, economic growth, including growing consumer spending, is still largely attributable to high oil prices.

While their rate of growth is impressive, the six GCC economies are still small by international standards. Their combined GDP of over US$600 billion constitutes just 5 percent that of the US or 22 percent that of Germany; similarly, their total population of 35 million amounts to 12 percent of the US's or 43 percent of Germany's. In world terms, this puts the GCC in the same league as Australia or the Netherlands.

Population growth is high, however, and leads to a young population: 61 percent of Saudi Arabia's population is under 25 years old, compared with 50 percent of India's, 39 percent of China's, and 30 percent of Europe's. A young working population is normally an asset, since it replenishes the public and private sectors and drives economic growth, but the youth of the GCC face a future of under- or unemployment as the region's education system has so far failed to equip them for the needs of the private sector.

Lots of "grow," not much "go"

If we try to measure the success of GCC companies by their stock market performance, we should proceed with caution. The region's capital markets are still young. Kuwait, the oldest market, was established in 1984; the UAE market was set up as recently as 2000. To be sure, the markets *seem* highly developed: their 2005 market capitalization exceeded that of the major emerging markets as a percentage of GDP, with the UAE scoring 185 percent and Saudi Arabia 208 percent, compared to 70 percent for India and 35 percent for China.[2] But other factors come into play: trading costs are higher than in mature markets, and investors are able to pursue only a limited range of investment strategies.

This raises questions about how efficient the market's pricing can be under such circumstances. In addition, many of the major players are government-held companies, so the stock markets can give us only a partial view: indeed, four of the world's 20 most valuable unlisted companies are from the GCC. What's more, the regulatory framework restricts international capital flows and the debt market is undeveloped. All of these factors limit the usefulness of capital market valuations as a yardstick of the success and failure of companies or industries.

There is one more fundamental difference between the GCC and more developed markets: because the economies – like others in Asia – are still developing rapidly, there has been practically no "go" in our "grow or go" equation. Since 2001, only a handful of companies have disappeared from the GCC stock market listings through liquidation.[3]

What all this means is that when we look at the performance of GCC companies, we see a very different landscape from that elsewhere. The youth of the stock markets precludes us from looking back further than five or ten years, and the period we can see may well not be representative. Conditions in the late 1990s when the oil price stood at US$10 or US$15 a barrel were very different to those today with prices at over US$60. Moreover, the number of listed companies has increased by 14 percent a year since the 1990s to today's total of 575, and market capitalization has increased roughly six-fold. Under these circumstances, we need to be careful about the conclusions we draw.

A sector view
What we can say with confidence is that in such a strong growth environment, it comes as no surprise that the stock market rewarded companies whose growth strategies enabled them to outgrow their competitors, and punished those that grew more slowly. Between 2001 and 2005, the top-quartile performers achieved returns of 100 percent a year, compared to 37 percent for the market as a whole, and 4 percent for the bottom quartile (Figure 3.1). In terms of revenues, the top-quartile companies grew by 22 percent, the

3.1 Performance of GCC companies
2001–05, percent

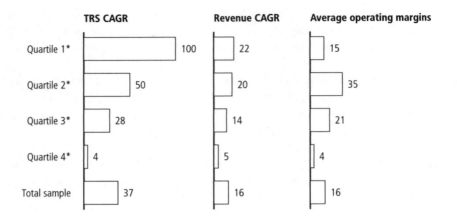

* On basis of TRS performance; median used to computate metrics
Source: Bloomberg; McKinsey analysis

market by 16 percent, and the bottom-quartile performers by 5 percent.[4] Not surprisingly, the best-performing sectors also showed the highest revenue growth. If you had investing in the building materials industry, a market that was growing at 25 percent a year, you would have reaped a return of 49 percent a year.

Let's now turn from our macro view of the economy and the stock market to look at the performance of specific sectors and companies.

Telecom
All the telecom companies in these six countries started from a similar place in that healthy growth in their home markets allowed them to grow organically and to grow revenues. Thus Saudi Telecom grew its revenues organically by 14 percent between 2000 and 2005, while Kuwait's Mobile Telecommunication Company (MTC) achieved 12 percent growth in its domestic operations over the same period.

However, it was clear from the outset that market growth would eventually slow down and deregulation would usher in new competitors that would take market share from incumbent players, increase pressure on prices, and squeeze margins. Those that felt the heat most were incumbents with small home markets such as MTC in Kuwait and Etisalat in the UAE. In response, they shifted their focus from organic growth at home to inorganic growth overseas.

MTC's push for international growth from 2003 onwards has led it to acquire businesses and licences not just elsewhere in the Middle East but in Africa too, where it is now present in 14 countries. By 2006, 80 percent of its revenues were derived outside Kuwait. If we look at its granular growth decomposition,[5] we can see that M&A contributed more than half of its growth in revenues since 1999 (Figure 3.2).

Etisalat has pursued a similar strategy. Since 2004 it has spent close to US$6 billion on licences and operations in Saudi Arabia, Egypt, Sudan, Afghanistan, Pakistan, and Central and West Africa, and plans further international expansion over the coming years.

The capital markets appear to have rewarded this aggressive international growth strategy, especially in MTC's case. Between 2001 and 2005, Etisalat delivered total shareholder returns of 34 percent, and MTC an even more impressive 46 percent.

3.2 MTC's granular growth decomposition
1999–2006

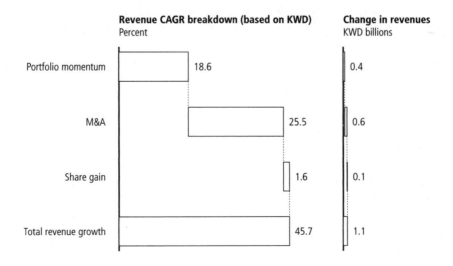

Source: Granular growth decomposition database

A different path was followed by Saudi Telecom (STC): namely, the pursuit of organic growth in its home market. As long as it benefitted from protection in its large and growing market, it was rewarded by strong capital market performance. Indeed, it was one of the ten most valuable telecom companies in the world at the end of 2005. However, its fortunes have taken a turn for the worse since then. Following market liberalization and the entry of Mobily into the mobile market, it has lost market share and suffered a decline in profits. The result: a halving of its market capitalization from US$80 billion in 2005 to US$40 billion in 2007.

Banking

By and large, this sector's stock price performance has been in line with that of the market as a whole, with a median TRS of 41 percent compared to the market median of 37 percent. Unlike telecom, where incumbents started from a monopoly position, banking has been a fragmented industry from the beginning, and even today market concentration is fairly low. The average market share for the top three players in the GCC as a whole is just 56 percent, although there is considerable variation between countries, with the UAE at just 32 percent and Oman at 69 percent.[6] Again in contrast with the telecom industry, the story in banking is chiefly one of organic growth; acquisitions have not played a major role.

The growth in the banking industry has been driven by market growth of 14 percent CAGR between 2001 and 2005, well above real GDP growth. However, the most successful listed banks – Bank ALJazira, Dubai Islamic, and First Gulf Bank – all grew their revenues at a rate far above the market average between 2001 and 2005, achieving 45, 34, and 87 percent respectively. To capture this growth wave, banks have had to enter new markets within the industry: investment banking, consumer finance, asset management, and brokerage. Emirates Bank, for example, notched up a CAGR of 18 percent from 1999 to 2006 purely through organic growth. It has been turning its attention to the fast-growing retail market, which now constitutes 30 percent of its overall business portfolio, up from 12 percent in 1999.

As the growth in financial services starts to slow, we can expect the region's banks to embark on a path of inorganic growth. The recent merger of NBD and Emirates Bank may well start a trend for further consolidation – much needed if GCC banks are to compete internationally in growth hot spots such as wealth management and investment banking. The balance sheet of the entire GCC banking sector currently stands at around US$675 billion: half that of a big European bank like ABN Amro, with US$1,300 billion in 2006.

Oil and petrochemicals

This industry tells a very different story. None of the region's major oil companies is listed at a stock exchange, so it is difficult to evaluate their skill at value creation. But there is no doubt about the sector's massive economic impact: Saudi Aramco, Kuwait Petroleum Corporation, Abu Dhabi National Oil Company, and Qatar Petroleum are considered to be among the 20 most valuable non-listed companies in the world, and they all make substantial contributions to the funding and wealth creation in their respective countries.

Saudi Aramco's revenues are, of course, highly dependent on the oil price. During the late 1990s they fell as oil prices declined from US$20 to US$10–15; since 2000, they have grown from US$58 billion to US$150 billion. In terms of the "grow or go" framework, they were in the right industry at the right time, even if they did have little choice in the matter! They have yet to use their financial muscle to make substantial acquisitions, but this may change if they decide to try to capture more of the value lower down the value chain.

Airlines

Every GCC country has at least one airline: Saudi Airlines in Saudi Arabia, Gulf Air in Bahrain, Qatar Airways in Qatar, Oman Air in Oman, Kuwait Airways in Kuwait, and in the UAE, Emirates in Dubai and Etihad in Abu Dhabi. None of them is a listed company,[7] and none has been involved in major acquisitions of other airlines, in keeping with the wider global industry, which has seen little M&A between big players so far.

Growth in this industry has been primarily organic, with Emirates Airlines standing out from the rest. It began in 1985 with two leased planes serving three destinations. Today it has 100 aircraft and another 150 on order, which gives some indication of its aspirations to future growth. One of the fastest-growing airlines in the world, it is also one of the most profitable. Of the AED23 billion revenues it has added to its top line since 2000, AED16 billion came from increased market share and AED6 billion from the growth of the airline market as a whole. By constantly strengthening its network, it has ensured continuing improvement in its economies of scale. This model of organic growth is also supported by a strong brand name, with Emirates investing some US$300 million a year in brand development.

Real estate

This booming sector is very important to the economies of the GCC. In a highly fragmented market, Dubai-based EMAAR is the only major player listed on a stock exchange. It dominates the whole region, accounting for more than half of the combined market capitalization of all the GCC's real estate players, and achieved top-line growth of a staggering 76 percent a year between 2001 and 2006. Only 11 percent of this growth came from its few acquisitions (Hamptons Group in the UK, John Laing Homes in the US, and a joint venture with Turner Construction from the US); the rest derived primarily from growth in its Dubai home market.

However, the company is now striving to maintain its organic growth rates by venturing abroad. It has already started operations in Syria, Egypt, Morocco, India, Pakistan, Saudi Arabia, Jordan, and more recently Indonesia. It may well intend to follow the pattern set by the GCC telecom players, but if it does, it is likely to do so primarily through organic growth rather than acquisitions.

Aluminium

In the aluminium industry, major players such as Dubal and Alba have been steadily growing their global market share over the past ten years. Ranked twenty-second in the world in midstream production capacity in 1999, Dubal has since risen to sixth place, and clearly aspires to rise further. One bold step in that direction was the formation of Emirates Aluminium International, its recent alliance with Abu Dhabi's Mubadala to build smelters in the Middle East and Africa with a total capacity of more than 2 million tons a year (6 percent of current world capacity).

By 2020, GCC players are expected to command a joint global market share of 15 to 20 percent, up from less than 3 percent in the early 1990s. In the past, growth was driven by the organic expansion of their production facilities; more recently, they have entered into upstream joint ventures to secure access to strategic raw materials. As their focus becomes increasingly international, we can expect them to pursue a more aggressive acquisition path. Emirates Aluminium International is already investing in India and Guinea.

Predator or prey?

Much of the recent rapid growth for GCC companies has come from satisfying the region's long-pent-up demand. There seems to be plenty of scope for continued growth in GDP: a rapidly growing population boosts the size of the workforce as well as consumer spending, while the global energy shortage looks likely to keep oil prices high for the foreseeable future. Most sectors still offer significant growth opportunities. In the financial services industry, insurance and asset management are ripe for expansion; in telecom, new technology and increasing penetration will drive growth.

Yet despite the strong fundamentals and the opportunities, the days of relatively easy growth are over for many of the region's leading companies. Domestic markets are too small to allow them to continue their high-growth trajectory indefinitely. Growing beyond the rate of real GDP growth will become harder and more expensive. Companies seeking to continue their present rate of growth will have to raise their share of inorganic growth – a new and risky game for many.

This may be one reason why the capital markets don't seem especially optimistic about GCC companies' growth prospects. The forward price/earnings multiple, which is a rough indicator of companies' predicted growth, is in the range of 14 to 16 for Saudi Arabia and the UAE. Though in line with the S&P 500's multiple of 15, this is well below that of India or China even after the recent corrections in these markets.

While GCC companies strive to become predators for growth through acquisition, they risk ending up as prey themselves. If the attention of global players were to shift towards the region, and ownership structures and regulations were to allow acquisition by foreign companies, many of them could be vulnerable. They still have some way to go before their market value makes them true global champions. Even regional giants Etisalat and MTC have yet to feature in the top 25 global telecom companies, despite the impressive increase in their market value over the past few years. Things are much the same in banking, where the GCC's largest player by market capitalization would not figure among the top 50 listed banks worldwide.

Among listed companies, only SABIC in chemicals and EMAAR in real estate would be within the top 15 in their respective industries. The most valuable companies and the ones with the potential to become true global players – the national oil companies – aren't listed and have yet to show much interest in growing beyond their core business.

To succeed internationally, GCC companies will need to take three key steps:

Develop a business model that can be leveraged globally. This business model needs to build on home-grown strengths while standing up to the pressures of markets that are more challenging than their domestic market in terms of customer service, labor costs, and competitive intensity. Some GCC companies, among them Emirates Airlines, clearly have the ability to develop such a business model. Others have yet to prove that they can repeat their regional success on the international stage.

Develop a global organization in terms of corporate culture, performance management, and talent development. Performance management needs to become more transparent, objective, and independent of personal relationships. People from different cultural backgrounds need to feel comfortable in the organization and have access to equal opportunities for development. EMAAR, the Dubai-based real estate developer, is one company that is already moving in this direction, with the nationalities of its top management team reflecting the diverse nature of its business. The acquisitions of John Laing Homes, a private property development company in the United States, and UK realtor Hamptons International not only gives EMAAR access to the British and US markets but allows it to draw on John Laing's experience in real-estate development and Hamptons' expertise in marketing. The latter skills in particular will be critical for EMAAR as it expands into overseas markets where – unlike the situation at home – the supply of real estate greatly outstrips demand.

Master the art of M&A and become adept at integrating newly acquired businesses. M&A is set to become a key instrument in most growth strategies, and many GCC companies are well positioned financially to take advantage of it: they generate strong cash flows that allow them significant leverage. Though their stock market valuations are high by international standards, they are below those of their counterparts in most other emerging markets, so they will need to focus on managing investors if they want to use high valuation as an acquisition lever. We can expect to see significant changes in the M&A landscape in the years ahead. Activity has been relatively low thus far, with volumes amounting to roughly 2 percent of market capitalization, compared to 5–6 percent in more mature markets. Privately held companies have accounted for the lion's share of deals, but as publicly listed companies take an increasing interest in M&A, activity is likely to rise to a level approaching that elsewhere. As companies compete head to head for assets in the region,[8] deals will become more sophisticated, with more deal auctions, more share deals, and more debt financing.

■ ■ ■

As we look ahead, it's clear that GCC companies have several strategic options, each with its own mix of organic and inorganic growth. Some may succeed in becoming major players in their home country or region, protected against acquisition by strong performance or regulation. Domestic players can rely largely on organic growth, and will need to identify the most attractive market segments for future growth. Regional players will need to balance organic and inorganic growth, given that the markets are still fairly protected against major acquisitions by overseas companies and acquisitions alone are unlikely to lead to regional leadership.

Some companies will be prey for international players, creating a lot of shareholder value on the way. And some will succeed in becoming global players, either in a broad industry or in a niche.

NOTES

[1] The measurement of *real* GDP growth treats oil-price increases as inflation, which is technically accurate for oil-consuming countries. But because the GCC produces oil and exchanges it for US dollars, price increases represent extra income that is fed back into their economies. It is therefore useful to look at *nominal* as well as real GDP growth to understand wealth creation in these countries. Nominal GDP growth better explains the economy and thus is a better benchmark for capital market performance. However, real GDP growth is a better metric for growth in industries that don't benefit directly from increases in oil prices.

[2] Since 2005, the GCC's market capitalization has dropped substantially, so that it is now in line with such markets as the US (135 percent) and the UK (139 percent).

[3] They include food and beverages producer Tomoor Oman and Saudi Arabia's Takaful Insurance Company.

[4] One interesting manifestation of the weakness of the markets is that there was no obvious correlation between the margins of the top performers and their market valuation; in fact, the second quartile showed higher margins than the top quartile.

[5] See chapter 2 of *The Granularity of Growth* for an explanation of this tool.

[6] Market shares for the top three banking players in the remaining countries are Qatar 66 percent, Kuwait 67 percent, and Saudi Arabia 45 percent. (Figures for market share in Bahrain are not available.)

[7] Oman Air was de-listed from Muscat Securities Market in June 2007, as it plans to become a closed joint stock company.

[8] Banks from the GCC are already bidding against the likes of Citibank for others in the region.

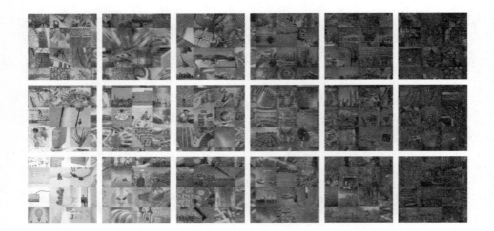

4

India: Creating winning enterprises in the private sector

Kuldeep Jain, Vivek Pandit, and Adil Zainulbhai

FOLLOWING THE ECONOMIC REFORMS it began in 1991, India has enjoyed more than a decade of powerful growth. Its GDP growth rate accelerated from 5.9 percent a year between 1995 and 2000 to 6.9 percent between 2000 and 2005, and now stands at more than 9 percent a year, making India one of the world's fastest-growing large economies.[1]

What's more, this rapid economic growth has paved the way for one of the world's most successful anti-poverty programs. The proportion of the population classified as deprived has been reduced from 93 percent in 1985 to around 54 percent today,[2] and is forecast to fall to 22 percent by 2025. This is a huge achievement: in effect, today's India has *431 million* fewer poor people than it would have had if poverty had remained at 1985 levels.

Four successive coalition governments have continued with economic reforms that have abolished licensing for manufactured goods, opened up most sectors to private participation, encouraged global fund-raising, and eased restrictions on international investment for Indian companies. At the same time, cuts in import tariffs and the opening up of large swathes of the economy to foreign investment have ushered in greater competition.[3]

India's impressive growth owes much to its dynamic and efficient private sector. Liberalization has freed it from former constraints, enabling it to improve its performance and overtake the government-owned companies that used to dominate the economy.

A comparison with China's private sector throws its significance into sharp relief. China has 14 private companies among its 100 most valuable companies; India has 80. China's private sector accounts for 6 percent of its top 100 companies' market capitalization and 3 percent of top 100 cumulative revenues; India's private sector accounts for 78 and 53 percent respectively.

The Indian private sector is also highly capital-efficient, particularly when compared to others in Asia. The reason is partly historical: between the 1970s and the reforms of the 1990s, it had to function in a capital-scarce economy and thus learned to manage its capital requirements efficiently. Another key factor was the country's comparatively well-developed stock markets, which put pressure on companies to sustain returns (Figure 4.1).

4.1 Outsize returns
ROIC for top 100 listed companies,* average for 2001–05, percent

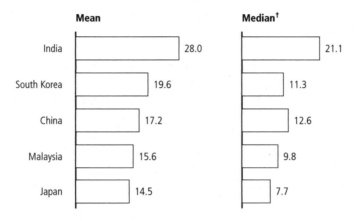

* By market capitalization (excluding financial institutions)
† Median is a good measure of central tendency when data points take extreme values
Source: McKinsey Corporate Performance Centre proprietary database

Grow, grow, grow

In order to gain a better understanding of how Indian companies grew and the strategies they used, we identified a set of 66 companies that featured among the top 100 companies by market capitalization and by revenue in 1993 and tracked their performance over the next two business cycles. The first, from 1993 to 1999, represents the period immediately after economic liberalization in 1992. The second, from 1999 to 2005, incorporates the global economic downturn of 2002–03 and the beginning of companies' emergence from it in 2005.

We classified the companies according to their performance in each cycle, using two yardsticks. We measured companies' **revenue growth** relative to gross output growth, taking our cut-off points as 14.9 percent in the first cycle and 12.2 percent in the second. We used gross output growth as a proxy for real GDP growth because it incorporates the effects of inflation, making it more compatible with corporate revenue figures. For our second yardstick, we took companies' **total returns to shareholders** relative to the market average, since TRS incorporates dividend payouts as well as capital gains. Here the cut-off point was set by the market average TRS: 7.8 percent in the first cycle and 13.4 percent in the second.

We ended up with four categories of performance. *Growth giants* met our thresholds for both growth and TRS; *performers* delivered high TRS but fell short on revenue growth; *unrewarded* companies delivered high revenue growth but fell short on TRS; and *challenged* companies fell short on both revenue growth and TRS.

The results of this analysis reveal that there is a clear correlation between growth and returns. Out of the 66 companies, 28 grew faster than India's gross output growth in the first cycle and produced an average TRS of 11.4 percent, earning returns 30 percent greater than the rest of the sample, which achieved a TRS of 8.6 percent.[4] However, only 11 of these 28 companies – or one in six of the overall sample – could be classified as growth giants, in that they were able to sustain growth over the entire cycle at above the rate of gross output growth as well as achieving higher than average shareholder returns.

In the second business cycle, the number dwindled further: only six of the original 11 companies maintained their growth giant status. Of the total sample, then, only one company in 11 managed to sustain above-average revenues and above-average shareholder returns across two business cycles (Figure 4.2).

4.2 It's hard to stay a growth giant

Cycle 1: 1993–99
Number of companies from total sample

Cycle 2: 1999–2005
Positions of cycle 1 growth giants

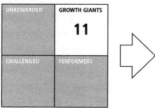

UNREWARDED	GROWTH GIANTS
11	
CHALLENGED	PERFORMERS

UNREWARDED	GROWTH GIANTS
2	**6**
CHALLENGED	PERFORMERS
2	**1**

EXIT
0

Source: Research Insight; Bloomberg; Datastream; McKinsey analysis

The message is clear: in India as elsewhere, past performance is no guarantee of future gains. Companies that manage to keep up their capital market performance in the longer term are the exception, not the rule. Unless they can sustain their lead by growing, their performance declines.[5] Staying still is not an option.

So what can companies do to ensure they capture the benefits of high economic growth and don't get left behind? Let's take a look at the Reliance Group, India's largest industrial conglomerate and one of the six growth giants that retained that distinction across two business cycles.

In 1993, at the start of the first business cycle we examined, the Reliance Group was focused primarily on downstream petrochemicals, a sector that had long sustained the company's high growth rate. However, it had already committed itself to constructing an oil refinery so as to move up the value chain. Not content with this first diversification, the group moved its flagship company Reliance Industries into three new and unrelated sectors: upstream oil and gas, retail fuel marketing, and biotechnology. To take advantage of two "hot spot" sectors, it also launched a mobile telecom subsidiary, Reliance Infocomm, and a power business, Reliance Power. It enjoyed strong tailwinds in both these businesses before eventually hiving them off in 2005 at a valuation of over US$12.5 billion.[6] In Reliance Industries' core business, meanwhile, the contribution of petroleum refining increased from just 1 percent of revenue in 1996 to around 56 percent in 2006 (Figure 4.3).[7]

4.3 Reliance's changing business mix

Net turnover, US$ million

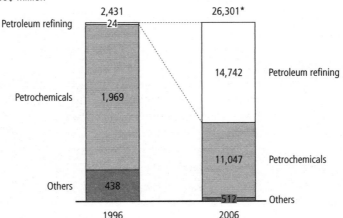

* Adjusted for inter-segment revenue transfer
Source: Annual reports

Reliance is committed to further substantial investments and diversifications. Between 2007 and 2012, the group intends to spend upwards of US$15 billion on adding a second oil refinery and investing in upstream gas exploration, significant retail investments and the development of special economic zones (multiple-use real-estate developments on the scale of small cities).[8]

Extraordinary transformations

One piece of good news to emerge from our analysis was that the fast pace of India's growth has enabled some companies to reshape their businesses and transform their performance. Against all expectations, some of the challenged companies in the first business cycle emerged to become a new generation of growth giants in the second. In most markets, by contrast, challenged companies were more likely to stay that way or to disappear than to achieve such a dramatic transformation. Of the 31 Indian companies that fell into the challenged category after the first business cycle, 11 became growth giants during the second. Nor were they the only companies to make a huge leap forward. Nine companies classified as unrewarded in the first cycle became growth giants in the second, as did three companies categorized as performers.

If we look at the eleven companies that metamorphosed from challenged to growth giants, we see that more than half of them came from India's two leading conglomerates: the Tata Group (Tata Steel, Tata Motors, Tata Power, Indian Hotels, and Voltas) and the Aditya Birla Group (Grasim and Aditya Nuvo). All were regarded as among India's better-managed corporations even before the 1991 economic reforms prompted them to increase their focus on cost and productivity. After emerging from this intense phase of activity at the end of the 1990s, they enjoyed a period of high growth and increased profitability. Let's examine three of the largest companies from these conglomerates to understand how they achieved their transformations.

In 1992, Tata Steel was a high-cost steel manufacturer. Accustomed to operating in a protected environment with high import tariffs, it had yet to invest in new technologies that would improve its efficiency. But as conditions became much more demanding over the years, it launched initiatives to cut manufacturing costs, improve its supply chain and integrate it with iron-ore supply, and revamp its organization structure. By 2003, these initiatives had made it one of the lowest-cost steel manufacturers in the world. More recently, its acquisition of Europe's Corus Steel made it the fifth-largest steel manufacturer in the world. It is currently investing in large greenfield facilities in the Indian states of Jharkhand, Chattisgarh, and Orissa.

Tata Motors took a different path: it moved segments to achieve higher growth. Primarily a commercial vehicles manufacturer, it entered the passenger car business in the 1990s, launching the Indica at a fraction of the usual cost involved in designing a new model. It also strengthened its mainstay business by acquiring Daewoo's heavy commercial vehicle business in Korea, which enabled it to expand its product line and launch Ace, a low-frills light commercial vehicle, at a significantly lower price. In addition, it has aggressively developed its auto parts venture TACO, its construction equipment business, and its finance arm as future growth engines.

Several companies from the Aditya Birla Group, most notably its flagship, Grasim, moved the center of gravity of their portfolios in this period. Faced with low growth in its mainstay business, viscose staple fibers, Grasim invested heavily in the cement business. Its first step was to acquire the cement business of Indian Rayon, another company in the group. It then bought a majority stake in L&T's cement business, now renamed Ultratech. These steps made Grasim into one of the country's largest cement companies, and it remains a market leader in the fibers business.

What makes a growth giant?

In our analysis, we looked closely at the growth giants to see how they managed to sustain high growth and profitability. We found they tended to do four key things:

- Rethink where to compete
- Leverage intellectual capital at significantly lower costs
- Innovate to serve consumer markets
- Use M&A to globalize.

Rethinking where to compete

The single most important factor that makes a company a growth giant is its choice of industry. Being ahead of the game is critical when you are seeking to enter and exploit new industries and booming sectors.

The importance of rethinking where to compete emerges starkly if we look at companies that weren't significant players in 1993 but have since grown to break into the list of the most valuable Indian corporations. Many of these companies have been operating in their current form for less than a dozen years. Three examples – ICICI Bank, Jet Airways, and Bharti Telecom – serve to illustrate how these companies made their transitions.

In the 1990s, ICICI Bank was the second-largest lender to industry in India.[9] However, the economic reforms that opened up the market to global forces had drastic consequences for the bank's loan portfolio. Managing director K. V. Kamath recalls, "Our core franchise was crumbling and we were right on the edge, so we had to reinvent ourselves."[10] ICICI's response was to refocus its services and grow its retail portfolio. Today it is among India's largest players in home loans, auto loans, and credit cards.[11]

To grow its retail portfolio, ICICI invested heavily in systems that allowed it to monitor the risks in consumer lending and manage a network of distributors in loans. It also used new technology to reduce its costs and enhance its profitability, introducing online trading with seamless connections between banking, depository, and brokerage, as well as using ATMs and internet technology in retail banking. Its technology costs are now just 10 percent of those of most other international banks, putting it in a good position both to develop its operations overseas[12] – something it has successfully done by starting from a base of Indian corporations and expatriates – and to expand into the broader retail market.

ICICI has spun off several of its successful new operations, including insurance, private equity, real estate, and back-office processing, into a separate holding company, ICICI Financial Services, which is currently valued at US$11 billion. The parent company is valued at US$25 billion.[13]

The story of Jet Airways is that of a business that has successfully moved industries. In the early 1990s, Jet was not an airline but one of India's largest and best-run ticketing agents. Once the airline industry was deregulated it became one of many new entrants, but quickly differentiated itself through its control of costs and quality of service. As other private airlines fell by the wayside, it emerged as the sole competitor to state-run Indian Airlines. Between 1999 and 2005, Jet grew its market share from 32 to 42 percent.[14]

In 2005, the government introduced measures that cut the cost of air travel in India, prompting a slew of new airlines to enter the market and precipitating a boom in demand. Air travel has grown by 25 percent a year since then.[15]

Jet's subsequent path involves both inorganic and organic growth. It recently acquired Sahara Airlines and rebranded it as budget offering Jet Lite. On the organic side, it has expanded its operations overseas with routes to London, New York, Singapore, Malaysia, and Bangkok, and recently established an international hub in Brussels to take on European hub carriers such as Lufthansa and British Airways.

Now that the economics of the international airline industry look increasingly shaky, it remains to be seen whether Jet can compete effectively with larger airlines or whether it will once again reinvent itself.

Bharti Enterprises is among the brightest stars of the past decade, having transformed itself from a telephone manufacturer into a leading wireless services provider. Mobile telephony is one of the fastest-growing industries in India: the number of subscribers increased from around 3.5 million in 2000 to around 148 million by mid-2007, and is forecast to reach almost 300 million by 2012.[16]

After deregulation allowed competition to the state-owned telecom provider, Bharti acquired the mobile phone licence for New Delhi. Since then it has grown its business both organically and via acquisition while outsourcing equipment to global operators. This strategy has enabled it to carve out a leadership position and achieve an ROIC of 29.8 percent, making it one of India's ten most valuable companies.[17] The company continues to maintain its high-growth trajectory and is currently pursuing new opportunities in retail and agri-business.

Leveraging intellectual capital at low costs

India has built a worldwide reputation in offshoring thanks to four sources of advantage: a vast pool of well-educated but fairly low-paid graduates; a base of capable service providers; a strong business case (with a typical payback period of nine months for offshoring investments); and an early validation of the credibility of its business model from multinationals such as GE, Citibank, and BA.

Top service providers such as TCS, Infosys, and Wipro have played a crucial role in ensuring the critical mass and credibility of India's IT industry. Today their cash flows and market capitalizations are on a par with those of the world's top three global IT companies (EDS, Accenture, and CSC) (Figure 4.4). The sector makes a remarkable contribution to the economy, accounting for around 10 percent of the total increase in GDP between 2004 and 2007. The IT and BPO (business process outsourcing) industries employ more than 1.25 million people directly and employment continues to grow at a furious pace. In 2007, the three largest IT services companies had 230,000 engineers on their rolls.[18]

However, IT isn't the only sector to have benefited from India's intellectual capital. It has been just as important in the growth of pharmaceuticals, engineering, and other sectors.

4.4 The might of Indian IT companies
US$ billion

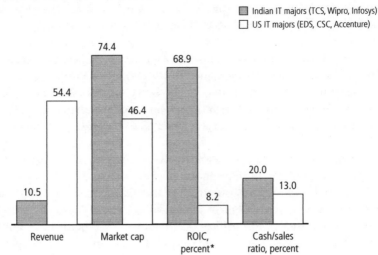

* ROIC of Accenture could not be calculated as it had negative invested capital
Source: Annual reports; McKinsey analysis

In pharmaceuticals, Indian companies have applied reverse-engineering to their product development process to tap into new areas, especially the exploding global generic pharmaceuticals market. The leader, Ranbaxy, is among the world's ten largest generics companies; other aspiring players such as Zydus Cadila, Sun Pharmaceuticals, and Cipla are following the same path, often using acquisition to establish global distribution capabilities. Of the top 25 generic pharma firms in the world, five are Indian.[19]

Many engineering-intensive industries, including auto components, machinery, and equipment manufacturing, have also taken advantage of the low-cost engineering and technical talent pool in India. When Crompton Greaves turned around its European acquisitions by offshoring its engineering and design work to India, it improved its targets' profitability from break-even to around 6 percent of sales.

Innovating to serve consumer markets
Companies that have innovated to serve consumer markets at scale include Nokia and such Korean companies as Hyundai, LG, and Samsung. They have created a virtuous cycle that typically has three components: superior price/value equation, large-scale production that achieves economies of scale, and extensive distribution systems.

Nokia has achieved a 70 percent market share in GSM mobile phones[20] by having two or three models at every price point and ensuring that customers believe it delivers great value. While its rivals focused on high-end technology to improve their products, Nokia tailored its products to the Indian market. Its innovations include a Hindi-language SMS and water-resistant phones. The company also strengthened its distribution network by providing extensive support to its dealers. Thanks to its overwhelming success in the Indian market, combined with other scale and factor advantages, it has been able to open a large manufacturing facility in Chennai.[21]

Another example is South Korean auto major Hyundai, which launched its Santro hatchback at a slightly higher price than rival models but with a superior value proposition. It made more than twenty modifications to the global Santro model to tailor it to local tastes and needs, and kept capital expenditure low by importing a mothballed plant from Canada and sourcing many components locally, a strategy that was economic only at high volumes. It also set up an extensive country-wide distribution network to boost sales and market share.

Using M&A to globalize
Indian companies are increasingly seeking to build global businesses by leveraging their advantages in domestic markets. The preferred business model has been to use M&A to achieve international expansion: overseas acquisitions have grown from less than US$1 billion in 2002 to a predicted more than US$30 billion in 2007.

Many companies reinvent themselves as they venture abroad. Suzlon transformed itself from a textiles firm into one of the world's top energy and wind-farm operations. Today its main businesses are setting up large wind-farm projects for investors and manufacturing wind turbines. It has invested over US$1.5 billion in international acquisitions in the past few years and has a global R&D and manufacturing footprint. Recently it hired a former GE executive as CEO, located new R&D facilities in Europe, and extended its manufacturing across Europe and Asia.[22]

Bharat Forge echoes Suzlon's success. Formerly a domestic supplier to Tata Motors, India's largest truck manufacturer, it has become the world's second-largest forging company.[23] To attain this position, it invested in export-oriented facilities in its home market and embarked on a cluster of acquisitions and joint ventures, including CDP and CDP Aluminiumtechnik in Germany, Federal Forge in the US, Imatra Forgings in Sweden, and FAW Forgings in

China.[24] These acquisitions are likely to prove crucial in establishing the company's global footprint and building relationships that can be gradually used to sell more products from the Indian base.

Suzlon and Bharat Forge are part of a growing trend that also includes Tata Steel's purchase of Corus and Hindalco's acquisition of Novelis. The scale of overseas investments has grown significantly since liberalization in 1991, and is expected to continue to do so as Indian companies pursue global business opportunities. Indeed, these investments are forecast to overtake inward-bound investments in 2007.

So much for the growth giants – but what about less successful companies?

Trapped in slow-growth sectors

Our analysis showed that in low-growth businesses, even well-managed companies fail to deliver shareholder returns. Two sectors plagued by low growth are the tyre industry (represented by MRF and JK in our sample) and packaged goods (HLL, Britannia, Colgate, ICI). Even though these companies enjoy very high returns on capital, they experienced lower revenue growth and shareholder returns in the second business cycle (Figure 4.5).

4.5 Slow growers in the second cycle

Percent

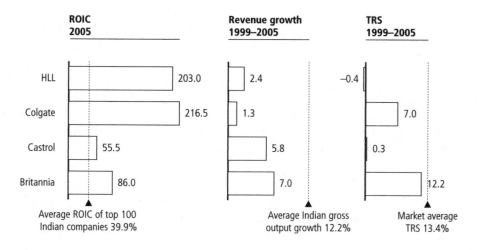

	ROIC 2005	Revenue growth 1999–2005	TRS 1999–2005
HLL	203.0	2.4	−0.4
Colgate	216.5	1.3	7.0
Castrol	55.5	5.8	0.3
Britannia	86.0	7.0	12.2

Average ROIC of top 100 Indian companies 39.9%

Average Indian gross output growth 12.2%

Market average TRS 13.4%

Source: McKinsey Corporate Performance Centre proprietary database

Most of these companies were once seen as exemplary. In the mid-1990s, Colgate and HLL achieved above-average TRS and revenue growth and qualified as growth giants. They are still regarded as possessing high-caliber management today. Yet their continuing focus on working very hard within their chosen business segment is not paying off. Their portfolios span foods and basic consumer products like soap and detergents where market penetration is high and growth comparatively low. These companies haven't actively sought out growth hot spots, and so haven't been well positioned to catch the next tailwind when it arrives.

Hindustan Unilever offers an example of a company that has neither moved to catch future growth tailwinds nor sought out opportunities for inorganic growth. Instead, it has persevered in its three core segments of home and personal care, foods, and specialty exports. In 1998, at the end of the first business cycle, it was the second most valuable company in India and one of its most respected corporations. Today it has lost some of its luster. Its average portfolio market growth is well below gross output growth at around 3.7 percent, while new domestic and multinational competitors continue to chip away at its markets and its talent.[25] Though it once boasted India's second-highest market capitalization, it is now fourteenth on the list and no longer the dominant force it was.[26]

The implications are stark. Companies whose markets are likely to grow more slowly than the overall economy need actively to explore new growth avenues beyond their core if they are to remain vibrant.

Little M&A-driven consolidation

Of the 66 companies we studied, only three no longer exist. We can largely attribute this to the limited role of M&A in India, which stems from three key factors:

- **The potency of growth.** Because most of India's markets have been growing so rapidly, few companies have needed to look to M&A as a source of extra growth. The rare exceptions are when a particular industry faces special circumstances, or when an acquirer wishes to move into a fast-growing segment. In the telecom industry, Bharti has made acquisitions in specific locations to complete its geographical footprint. Reliance Industries moved into power by buying into BSES, renaming it Reliance Power, and then growing the business at a furious pace. In cement, Holcim acquired ACC and subsequently Ambuja Cements to become a leading player commanding more than a quarter of the market.[27]

- **Regulatory barriers and government ownership prevent acquisition** in certain industries such as banking, petroleum, and telecom. In our 1993 sample, 11 of the 66 companies were government owned. Although M&A is theoretically permitted in banking, the voting rights of any shareholder are capped at 10 percent irrespective of the size of their stake,[28] which has deterred acquisitions of private-sector banks. But most of the industry – representing three-quarters of deposits – is still controlled by the public sector and the government is unwilling to sell.[29] In downstream petroleum, around 85 percent of retailing is in the hands of three government-owned corporations: Indian Oil (IOC), Bharat Petroleum (BPCL), and Hindustan Petroleum (HPCL).[30] While downstream retailing is open to any company that has invested in excess of US$500 million in India's petroleum industry, regulatory hurdles prevent such investments and leave global giants such as Shell and BP on the sidelines. In telecom, the government prohibits a merged entity from having more than 67 per cent of the market in a telecom circle (typically a state), thereby preventing market leaders from consolidating the industry.[31]

- **Hostile bids and leveraged buyouts are discouraged.** Two factors make hostile acquisitions difficult in India. First, the level of shareholding required to block the special resolutions[32] that are required for most significant corporate decisions is only 26 percent, rather than a majority of 51 percent. Second, large government-owned financial institutions such as UTI (a mutual fund) and LIC (Life Insurance Corporation of India) typically own a shareholding of 10 to 20 percent in many large corporations and tend to endorse the actions of the promoters unless they have a poor history of delivering shareholder returns or there are other special circumstances. Nor does the government permit financial leverage in aggressive takeovers. As a result, acquisitions that would produce more efficient capital structures don't take place in India.

However, recently, the role of M&A, both domestic and international, has been growing in importance and the inorganic route will definitely be a more prominent vehicle for growth in the future.

Tremendous opportunities driven by economic growth

Forecasts suggest that India's real compound annual growth rate will step up a notch between 2005 and 2025 to 7.3 percent,[33] a big increase on the previous two decades' rate of 6 percent. This will lead to an almost three-fold increase in average real household disposable incomes from Rs113,744 in 2005 to Rs318,896 by 2025, a CAGR of 5.3 percent (up from 3.6 percent). The middle class[34] will grow enormously as a result: from about 5 percent of the population (13 million households or 50 million people) in 2005 to an expected 41 percent of the population (128 million households or 583 million people) in 2025. Companies seeking to tap into opportunities created by India's economic growth should bear several things in mind:

"Where to compete" choices are key

Increasing spending power will prompt a shift in consumption patterns. The middle class already account for 18 percent of total consumption; this is likely to rise to 59 percent by 2025. India's consumers constitute the twelfth largest market in the world today, but by 2025, they will rank as the fifth largest. Indian companies and overseas investors alike will need to channel their investments appropriately to capture the resulting growth in consumption.

India's market growth will open up many opportunities, but companies need to be aware that consumption patterns are shifting away from necessities such as food and beverages, apparel, and housing towards personal products, transportation, communication, education, recreation, and healthcare. Companies need to monitor expected growth in industry segments so that they can constantly reassess where they compete (Figure 4.6).

4.6 Shifting spending patterns

Average personal household consumption, percent, INR thousand (2000)

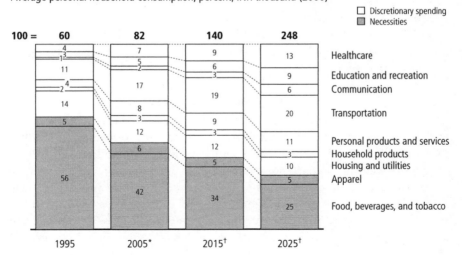

Numbers do not always add up to 100% because of rounding
* Esitmated
† Forecast
Source: *The "Bird of Gold": The Rise of India's Consumer Market*, McKinsey Global Institute, May 2007

Several companies are already making substantial strides in nascent sectors. Fortis Healthcare (a sister company of Ranbaxy) and Apollo Hospitals are both expanding rapidly in healthcare, and particularly in the health provider segment. Fortis Healthcare was launched only a few years ago but has grown rapidly through acquisitions and joint ventures, having acquired India's most renowned heart hospital, formed partnerships with several hospital-operating trusts, and made an agreement with the country's biggest land developer, DLF, to build and operate hospitals in around 30 cities over the next few years.[35] Funding for these expansions has been raised through a mix of promoter equity, private equity, and a public issue. The company has already achieved a market capitalization of US$482 million.[36]

The government's decision to substitute regulators for direct ministerial control in certain industries including power, oil, and financial services is likely to accelerate competition, boosting productivity and overall growth and hence encouraging increased participation from multinationals. Meanwhile, many of India's private industries will remain fragmented while witnessing very high levels of competition, increasing the pressures for consolidation.

This pressure is especially evident in aviation and telecom. India currently has five or six airlines per short-haul route, making it one of the most competitive aviation industries in the world even though its passenger volume is a fraction – just over a tenth – of US traffic.[37] There are already moves towards industry consolidation. Jet Airways has bought Sahara Airlines and Kingfisher has acquired a substantial stake in Air Deccan in a bid to improve profitability in a difficult industry. In telecom, India has five players in most circles, and seven or eight in some – much higher than the global average of two or three players per region.

Globalization will be a priority for Indian corporations

Though growth at home will be strong, the hunger for yet more growth will ensure that globalization remains a priority for many companies. In a 2007 McKinsey survey carried out at the Confederation of Indian Industry forum, over 65 percent of the participants rated globalization as one of the priority areas for their company. Around 60 percent said they had just begun their globalization journey or were about to do so. Most companies recognized they face challenges, and thought the most important were developing the ability to integrate their acquisitions and managing their global talent pool (rated as the biggest challenges by 40 and 33 percent respectively).

We can expect several different globalization models to emerge, depending on the rationales of the acquirers:

- Gaining international access to channels that can create cross-selling opportunities. Indian companies use this model to capture two benefits: increased sales and cost savings from leveraging their cost advantages in procurement, manufacturing, and services. Over 80 percent of M&A fits this category in industries as varied as generic pharmaceuticals, chemicals, auto component manufacturing, engineering goods, IT services, and BPO.

- Filling a gap in the product line or supply chain. Software company Wipro paid US$93 million for Spectramind in 2002 in order to enter the BPO space, and has recently acquired Saraware to fill the gap in its telecom portfolio. Similarly, Suzlon acquired Hansen Transmissions, one of the world's largest turbine gearbox manufacturers, to gain control of this critical component.[38]

- Acquiring supplies of natural resources. Tata Power invested US$1.1 billion in a 30 percent stake in P. T. Arutmin and P. T. Kaltim Prima Coal to secure future coal supplies for its 7,000 mw power plants under construction on the west coast of India.[39] Similarly, petroleum major ONGC made investments totalling US$1.4 billion in 2005–06 to acquire upstream assets.[40]

Multinationals should start building brands and skills

India's economic expansion offers significant growth opportunities for multinationals. Some have already become an integral part of India's growth story, among them Citigroup, Hindustan Lever, ITC, Hutchison Whampoa, LG Electronics, Samsung, Holcim, IBM, Nokia, and Suzuki.[41] We can identify several characteristics common to all of them:

- They set high aspirations for India, backed by long-term commitment from their global leaders.

- They rely extensively on local management teams, building strong teams of Indian executives while drawing on global support in areas such as R&D and marketing.

- They have adapted their business models to local conditions rather than simply importing models wholesale from overseas.

- They try not to rely on joint ventures unless they have to use them to access privileged assets (in which case they ensure they retain management control).

GE's CEO, Jeffrey Immelt, had some interesting things to say about how multinationals should adapt to succeed at a local level: "Globalization is entering a fourth stage. It started out importing high-end products from the United States to India, then turned to local joint ventures, followed by moves to build factories in China and India, its current focus. The next stage is designing technologies in India for the rest of the world."[42]

■ ■ ■

The Indian corporate sector's journey since liberalization has been like a pendulum swinging from early euphoria to the sober realization that lower tariff barriers demanded substantial performance improvements, and then back to euphoria again as the quickening pace of economic expansion opens up many more opportunities. Along the way, lessons have been learned from successes and failures alike. Future winners will need to couple an instinct for where to locate new market opportunities with the ability to build a company capable of executing and thriving in a highly competitive market. As we look back on the first 15 years of liberalization, we can predict that the next 15 will be just as eventful a period in India's corporate story.

NOTES

[1]   Central Statistical Organisation (CSO), India.

[2]   McKinsey Global Institute, May 2007, *The "Bird of Gold": The Rise of India's Consumer Market*. The definition of poverty – the deprived segment – as households with less than 90,000 Indian rupees of annual disposable income is also the measure used by the National Council for Applied Economic Research (NCAER). The government's official definition of poverty is based on calorie intake and is set at 2,400 calories per capita per day in urban areas and 2,100 calories per capita per day in rural areas. According to this lower threshold, extreme poverty dropped from 36 per cent of the population in 1993 to 29 percent in 1999.

[3]   Prior to liberalization, import tariffs were very high: the top rate was 400 percent and rates of between 110 and 150 percent applied to many goods. By 2001, the average rate had dropped to 25 percent (Arvind Panagariya, *India's Economic Reforms: What has been accomplished? What remains to be done?*, Asian Development Bank, ERD Policy Brief Series, February 2002).

[4]   Bloomberg; Research Insight; Datastream; McKinsey analysis

[5]   India differs from the developed economies in that growth is not a clear predictor of survival, perhaps because the market for M&A is not as well developed as it is in the US, Europe, and Australia.

[6]   Dealogic; M&A database; press reports.

[7]   Annual reports.

[8]   Real estate development for multiple uses at the scale of a mini city

[9]   "ICICI 97–98 1st half disbursals up," Reuters, October 1997.

[10] Leo Puri, "The CEO as CIO: An interview with the head of India's top private bank", *The McKinsey Quarterly*, March 2007, p. 4.

[11] "ICICI Bank: Crossing the Rubicon," SSKI India Research, 2007.

[12] Leo Puri, "The CEO as CIO: An interview with the head of India's top private bank", *The McKinsey Quarterly*, March 2007, p. 6.

[13] "ICICI to set aside 5% of issue for existing shareholders," *Financial Express*, 14 June 2007.

[14] "India business insight," *Business World*, 3 April 2006; *Economic Times*, 26 November 1999.

[15] www.indianairports.com, 13 August 2007.

[16] International Telecommunications Union; World Bank; trade sources; Euromonitor International.

[17] ROIC was calculated for the year 2006.

[18] National Association of Software and Service Companies.

[19] World Generic Markets Report, 2007.

[20] "MNC no. 1," *Business India*, 12 August 2007.

[21] Nokia website.

[22] Press release, 29 January 2007.

[23] Parent company website, www.kalyanigroup.com.

[24] Dealogic; www.bharatforge.com.

[25] Dealogic; analyst reports; McKinsey analysis.

[26] Datastream.

[27] "Gujarat Ambuja Cements: Holcim's gateway to India," *The Hindu*, 5 February 2006.

[28] Banking Regulation Act 1949, as quoted in "Shareholder moves court against merger of LKB," *The Hindu*, 19 October 2006.

[29] Reserve Bank of India guidelines as quoted in Dun & Bradstreet, *Overview of the Banking Industry*, 2007.

[30] PFC Energy, *Country Profile India*, 2005.

[31] "Catch in telecom intra-circle merger norms," *Financial Express*, 3 March 2004.

[32] Special shareholder resolutions are required for most major corporate decisions such as M&A and new investments.

[33] The forecast is derived from a macroeconomic model developed by Oxford Economics.

[34] The definition of middle class used here is households with real annual disposable income between Rs200,000 (US$5,000) and Rs1,000,000 (US$25,000).

[35] "DLF to doctor you with Fortis," *Economic Times*, 1 June 2007.

[36] Bloomberg.

[37] Ministry of Civil Aviation; Airport Authority of India; Bureau of Transportation.

[38] Dealogic database.

[39] www.tatapower.com.

[40] www.infraline.com.

[41] Nigel Manson, Shirish Sankhe, and Kuldeep Jain, "The right passage to India," *McKinsey on Finance*, February 2005.

[42] "Globalization is a tough sell, GE's Immelt says," Reuters, 6 July 2007.

5

Japan: From bubble to bust and back again

Peter Kenevan

THE PAST 20 YEARS have been turbulent times for the Japanese economy. First came the bubble economy of the late 1980s, which saw stock prices balloon, real-estate values soar, and speculation become rife. While underlying real GDP grew at an average 5 percent,[1] the Nikkei index rose at an annualized rate of nearly 30 percent, increasing from ¥11,545 in January 1985 to ¥38,915 at the end of December 1989. Total stock market capitalization[2] almost tripled from less than ¥200 trillion in December 1985 to a peak of ¥591 trillion by the end of December 1989.[3] Underlying the rapid growth in the equity markets was a real-estate bubble. The total value of real estate grew at an annual CAGR of nearly 20 percent, from ¥1,060 trillion in 1985 to ¥2,452 trillion in 1990 (Figure 5.1).[4]

But then the bubble burst, sending Japan spiralling into the traumatic and recessionary lost decade of the 1990s. The Nikkei fell from its peak of ¥38,915 in December 1989 to ¥20,221 by October 1990, and continued to drift downward for the next ten years, reaching a low of ¥7,607 in April

5.1 Turbulent times

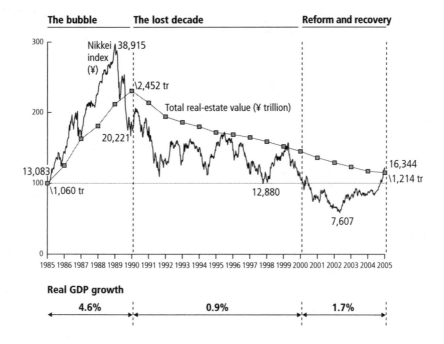

Source: Nikkei Shinbun; Bloomberg; Datastream; annual report on National Accounts (2005); McKinsey analysis

2003. Total market capitalization during this period fell by more than 60 percent to a low of ¥228 trillion in April 2003; similarly, real-estate values fell by 47 percent from their 1990 peak of ¥2,452 trillion to a low of ¥1299 trillion in 2003.[5] Between 1991 and 2001, underlying real GDP growth averaged less than 1 percent a year. The economy was in desperate trouble: consumers cut back spending, companies struggled in a deflationary environment, and the banking system was overloaded with bad debt and impaired collateral.

From the mid-1990s onwards, Japanese regulators began responding to the threats of deflation with a series of financial reforms that included lifting foreign-exchange and insurance-rate restrictions and allowing the formation of bank holding companies. The reforms, known as the "Big Bang," gathered momentum after 2001 when the Koizumi administration took steps to unblock the banking system by subsidizing the write-off of bad loans and started to push hard for the sale and restructuring of troubled companies.[6] As the reforms gathered pace, the administration launched the difficult and still ongoing process of privatizing some of the largest and most problematic state-owned enterprises, including the Japan Highway Public Corporation and Japan Post.

These reforms received a boost from Japan's booming trade with China, which grew from ¥5.4 trillion (exports plus imports) in 1995 to ¥20.8 trillion in 2005.[7] Thanks to the reforms and the tailwind provided by global economic growth, nominal GDP growth snapped back to about 2 percent a year from 2001. Meanwhile, the Nikkei recovered from its low of ¥7,607 in April 2003 to reach ¥16,000 by December 2005, with total market capitalization more than doubling to ¥550 trillion.

The performers create the value

The traumas of the past 20 years have accelerated the dismantling of Japan Inc. as well as stress-testing Japanese companies. Through these difficult years the companies with the best chance of survival have been those that have kept growing in excess of GDP – even though they have not necessarily been the best at rewarding shareholders.

To assess the performance of Japanese companies, we looked at the 57 largest companies in Japan by market capitalization and revenue as of 1987 and tracked their growth (relative to nominal GDP growth) and TRS performance (relative to the market average) across two business cycles, 1987 to 1996 and 1996 to 2005.

It's worth noting that over the past two business cycles Japanese companies as a whole have performed miserably compared with those in most other countries. In the US, Australia, Hong Kong, and India, companies that grew faster than GDP during the first business cycle delivered a median annual TRS of 10 to 15 percent across both business cycles, compared with just 2 percent in Japan. Indeed, even companies that grew more *slowly* than GDP during the first cycle in these four countries managed to deliver median TRS of 5 to 10 percent a year averaged across both cycles, whereas Japan's slow growers actually *destroyed* shareholder value at a median rate of –1 percent (Figure 5.2).

5.2 A dismal showing
Large-company averages

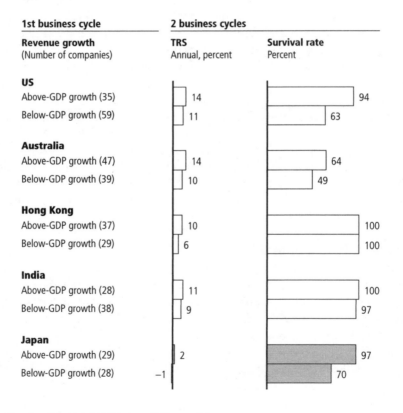

1st business cycle	2 business cycles	
Revenue growth (Number of companies)	**TRS** Annual, percent	**Survival rate** Percent
US		
Above-GDP growth (35)	14	94
Below-GDP growth (59)	11	63
Australia		
Above-GDP growth (47)	14	64
Below-GDP growth (39)	10	49
Hong Kong		
Above-GDP growth (37)	10	100
Below-GDP growth (29)	6	100
India		
Above-GDP growth (28)	11	100
Below-GDP growth (38)	9	97
Japan		
Above-GDP growth (29)	2	97
Below-GDP growth (28)	–1	70

Source: Bloomberg; Research Insight; Datastream; McKinsey analysis

Let's now look at the performance of the companies in our sample during the first business cycle, 1987 to 1996. Our yardsticks were whether they grew at above or below the nominal GDP growth of 3.8 percent, and whether they generated above or below the market average TRS of –1.05 percent. After removing one company that exited during the cycle, we were left with 56 companies at the end: 21 growth giants, 12 performers, 8 unrewarded, and 15 challenged. Figure 5.3 shows these results as a percentage share of the overall sample.

5.3 The growth performance matrix

Share of sample by category based on 1987–96 performance

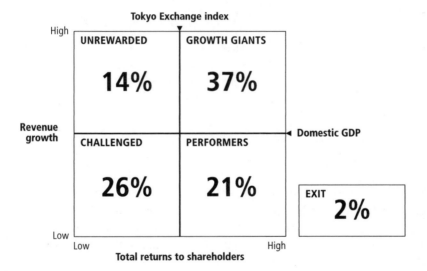

Source: Bloomberg; Research Insight; Datastream; McKinsey analysis

The picture changes in the course of the second business cycle. In general, the *growth giants* carry on growing, but nearly half of them don't get credit for it from the markets. Out of 21 growth giants at the end of the first business cycle, just nine remained growth giants at the end of the second cycle, while eight dropped into the unrewarded category, one became a performer, two were challenged, and one had exited (Figure 5.4).

5.4 The growth giants

How they fared in the second cycle

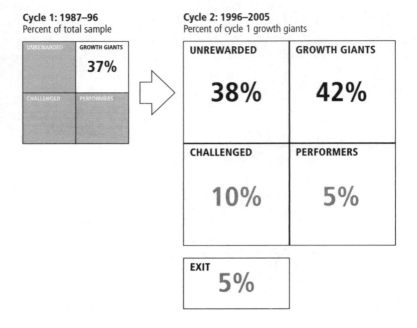

Cycle 1: 1987–96
Percent of total sample

| UNREWARDED | GROWTH GIANTS 37% |
| CHALLENGED | PERFORMERS |

Cycle 2: 1996–2005
Percent of cycle 1 growth giants

UNREWARDED	GROWTH GIANTS
38%	42%
CHALLENGED	PERFORMERS
10%	5%

| EXIT |
| 5% |

Source: Bloomberg; Research Insight; Datastream; McKinsey analysis

Japan was unlike other markets in that many companies stayed in the *performer* category for two consecutive business cycles. This unusual trend is driven in part by the low bar for TRS performance and the substantial scope for additional corporate restructuring in Japan, but also by the fact that many of these companies are from the highly regulated electric power industry, as we see later. Out of 12 performers at the end of the first cycle, five remained performers at the end of the second cycle, three were able to restart growth and become growth giants, one was unrewarded, and three had exited (Figure 5.5).

The eight *unrewarded* companies continued to disappoint shareholders through the second business cycle, with three remaining in the unrewarded category and three falling into the challenged category. Yet two of them bucked the trend, one by becoming a growth giant and one a performer; none was forced to exit (Figure 5.6).

5.5 The performers

How they fared in the second cycle

Cycle 1: 1987–96
Percent of total sample

UNREWARDED	GROWTH GIANTS
CHALLENGED	**PERFORMERS** 21%

Cycle 2: 1996–2005
Percent of cycle 1 performers

UNREWARDED	GROWTH GIANTS
8%	25%
CHALLENGED	PERFORMERS
0%	**42%**

EXIT
25%

Source: Bloomberg; Research Insight;
Datastream; McKinsey analysis

5.6 The unrewarded

How they fared in the second cycle

Cycle 1: 1987–96
Percent of total sample

UNREWARDED 14%	GROWTH GIANTS
CHALLENGED	PERFORMERS

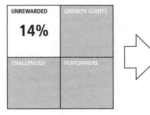

Cycle 2: 1996–2005
Percent of cycle 1 unrewarded

UNREWARDED	GROWTH GIANTS
37%	13%
CHALLENGED	PERFORMERS
37%	13%

EXIT
0%

Source: Bloomberg; Research Insight;
Datastream; McKinsey analysis

The story was very different for the *challenged* companies, for whom it was make or break in the second cycle. Out of the 15 companies that were challenged at the end of the first business cycle, seven managed to transform themselves into growth giants, but five were forced out of the market altogether (Figure 5.7).

5.7 The challenged
How they fared in the second cycle

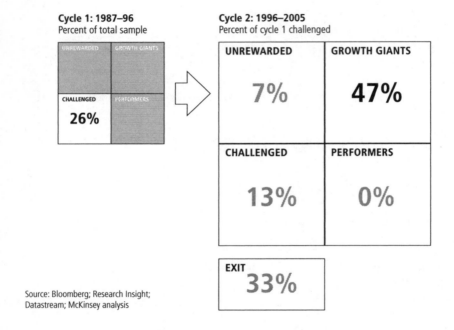

Cycle 1: 1987–96
Percent of total sample

| UNREWARDED | GROWTH GIANTS |
| CHALLENGED 26% | PERFORMERS |

Cycle 2: 1996–2005
Percent of cycle 1 challenged

UNREWARDED	GROWTH GIANTS
7%	**47%**
CHALLENGED	PERFORMERS
13%	0%

EXIT
33%

Source: Bloomberg; Research Insight;
Datastream; McKinsey analysis

By the end of the second business cycle, nine companies have exited and we are left with 47 companies: 20 growth giants, seven performers, 13 unrewarded, and seven challenged.

Among the countries we examined, Japan was unique in that first-cycle growth was a strong predictor of survival (of 29 companies that grew in excess of GDP in the first business cycle, 28 remained at the end of the second cycle), but a less reliable predictor of sustained shareholder value creation (of these same 29 companies, 16 delivered below-average TRS in the second cycle). The group most likely to reward shareholders in the second business cycle was not in fact the first-cycle growth giants, but rather the performers.

Scrutinizing sectors

In Japan as in other countries we examined, companies in some sectors tend to do better than those in others because growth and performance challenges and opportunities differ significantly by sector. Using our granular growth decomposition database, we analyzed a range of companies from various sectors to understand how growth and TRS performance compare within and across sectors, and to assess whether growth is coming from portfolio momentum, M&A, or market-share gain.

Auto manufacturers: An organic road to success

Japan's leading automobile manufacturers have had a great 20 years; all those in our survey (Toyota, Nissan, Honda, and Denso) qualified as growth giants in both business cycles. A granular look at how they grew reveals that in spite of their very different ownership and management cultures, Toyota and Nissan have achieved their success through similar strategies: rapid organic growth and market-share gains on a global scale.

Toyota grew its revenues by an average of 7.5 percent a year between 1999 and 2005, adding 2.8 million unit sales. The company, which is deeply committed to preserving its unique corporate culture, drove its growth almost entirely organically: most came from market-share gains (2 million units), with underlying market growth accounting for the remainder (0.8 million units). Domestic growth accounted for just 0.2 million units; the rest came from North America (0.9 million units), Asia (1 million units), Europe (0.4 million units), and other markets (0.3 million units).

This overseas growth was reinforced by the addition of overseas capacity: Toyota established several new factories in China (with JV partners), the US, and Mexico, and announced plans to build additional new plants in the US and China as well as in Russia, Canada, and India. As of 2007, 75 percent of Toyota's total ¥24 trillion in revenues comes from outside its home market.

Unlike most of its major competitors, Toyota has significant investment in and tight operational links with its core suppliers, owning about 30 percent of the shares of each of its two major suppliers, Denso and Aishin Seiki. It sees this connection as a critical strength as the complexity of auto systems increases (electronics are expected to account for 40 percent of the average car's total value by 2015) and integration challenges grow. If Toyota engages in M&A in the future, it is likely to focus on strengthening or extending its presence vertically along the value chain rather than building scale horizontally.

In contrast, Nissan has become the poster-child for the regenerating role that foreign ownership and management can play in the Japanese economy. It came close to bankruptcy in the late 1990s, but was rescued by a strategic investment from Renault and the charismatic and effective turnaround leadership of Carlos Ghosn. Like Toyota, it has succeeded largely by grabbing market share from foreign rivals.

The company increased unit sales by a cumulative 1 million units between 1999 and 2005, growth of 6 percent a year. Underlying market growth was responsible for 30 percent of this growth and the remaining 70 percent came from market-share gains at competitors' expense. Like Toyota, Nissan now depends almost entirely on foreign markets for its growth: overseas sales accounted for 90 percent of growth in this period, while as of 2007 roughly 80 percent of its total ¥10.5 trillion revenues came from overseas. Between 1999 and 2005 Nissan opened new factories in China (with JV partners) and the US, and announced plans for a new factory to be opened in India in 2009.

Whereas Toyota seems likely to continue to go it alone in the global marketplace, Nissan has sought to leverage its relationship with parent Renault to grow in Europe, a market where it has historically been weak, as well as to enter China and other emerging markets.

High-tech conglomerates: Subscale behemoths

Most of Japan's high-tech giants delivered good growth and TRS performance during the first business cycle but declined dramatically during the second. They have struggled with fragmented business portfolios, very high levels of competition in the domestic market, and market-share losses to foreign competitors at a global level.

A glance at the landscape illustrates the challenges these companies are facing. Fujitsu suffered negative growth in both revenues and TRS from 1999 to 2004. Toshiba experienced flat revenues and negative TRS growth. Panasonic managed to grow by reconsolidating with its sister company Matsushita Electric Works, but recorded negative TRS growth.

A more granular look at the nature of these companies' organic growth illustrates an even more troubling picture. While the underlying markets for their various businesses have been growing steadily, this growth has been completely wiped out (in the case of Fujitsu and Panasonic) or largely offset (in the case of Toshiba) by their loss of market share across virtually all product categories.

The broader structural problems in the industry can be illustrated by the competitive situation in the cellphone market. There are currently nine domestic manufacturers competing for share in the stagnating domestic market (shipments actually fell from 47.6 million units in 2000 to 44.8 million in 2005).[8] Despite the flat market, conditions dictate that these players need to keep making substantial investments in developing Japan-specific phones.

Only Sony (through its Sony Ericsson joint venture) has been able to grow globally, achieving a global market share of 7 percent in 2005. All other Japanese cellphone manufacturers have negligible presence overseas, having experienced a rapid shrinkage in global market share from more than 5 percent of total unit sales in 1999 to just over 3 percent in 2005. NEC, the domestic market leader with a fifth of Japan's market in 2005, had just 1 percent of the global market at that time.[9]

The underlying problems faced by Japan's high-tech companies are underlined by the dilemma now confronting the fragmented and subscale semiconductor manufacturers, most of which are divisions or subsidiaries of high-tech conglomerates. They are seeking to introduce the latest generation of manufacturing equipment so as to stay competitive at a global level. A scale-efficient 300mm semiconductor fabrication plant needs to process at least 20,000 to 30,000 wafers a month, and to build a facility with this capacity costs roughly US$3 billion.[10]

Recognizing that most players lack the scale to justify making such an investment independently, policy makers at Japan's Ministry of Economics, Trade, and Industry (METI) have repeatedly tried to push the industry to co-invest in a "Rising Sun Foundry,"[11] but it has stubbornly resisted, and most manufacturers have gone ahead with their own investments. As of 2007, eight out of the twelve companies have built 300mm facilities (excluding test fabrication units), yet only three of them (all developed by memory-chip manufacturers) have the capacity to satisfy the necessary scale requirements.[12] Virtually all the other manufacturers are struggling with the poor economics created by their subscale and under-utilized facilities. Here again, a failure to consolidate the market, or even to collaborate, has left the high-tech industry with excess capacity overall but subscale businesses at the individual company level.

Despite the fragmentation of the market and the consequent drag on economics, few high-tech companies have used M&A to restructure and focus their portfolios. Inorganic activity was negligible between 1999 and 2005 with the exception of Panasonic's reconsolidation and the spin-off of the financing and logistics arms at Toshiba and Fujitsu.

While they were beating one another to death in the domestic marketplace, Japan's high-tech conglomerates were also losing ground globally. Between 1999 and 2005 Toshiba grew by only 5 percent in the US, 2.4 percent in Europe, and a mere 1 percent in fast-growing Asia. Panasonic's revenues for the same period were flat in the US and grew by only 3.5 percent in Europe and 5.2 percent in Asia. Meanwhile, Fujitsu actually managed to shrink by 14 percent in the US and 5 percent in Europe, though it managed to grow by 3.4 percent in Asia.

When we contrast the fate of Japan's high-tech conglomerates with their more focused and aggressive global competitors, the challenges become even starker. From 1999 to 2005, revenue growth for Toshiba, Panasonic, and Fujitsu was essentially flat, while their Asian rivals achieved rapid increases in their CAGR: Samsung by 20 percent, LG Electronics by 34 percent, Lenovo by 35 percent, and Huawei by 25 percent. Their more focused American competitors fared well too: Cisco and HP both grew by 13 percent.[13]

No major Japanese conglomerate has yet exited the high-tech industry, but slow growth, low profitability, poor capital efficiency, and abysmal TRS are major challenges in the face of ever tougher global competition.

Electric power companies: Will their luck hold?

Over the past two business cycles, most of Japan's electric power companies have performed well for shareholders, despite stagnant revenues. Four out of the five electric utilities in our survey (Kansai, Chubu, Kyushu, and Chugoku) were performers across both business cycles, and the fifth (Tokyo) transformed itself from challenged to growth giant. If we take a more granular look at the industry, though, we can see that they got a lot of help from regulators and market forces.

For most of the post-war period, Japan's major power companies benefited from a regulated and highly profitable oligopoly. In 2000, the regulators liberalized the market to allow competition, including new-entrant independent power producers (IPPs) for large accounts. The incumbents initially saw deregulation as a threat, but favorable market forces combined with their own discipline ensured that they prevailed: as of 2006, the new entrant IPPs had less than 2 percent of the overall market.[14]

There are several reasons for this somewhat surprising outcome. For a start, the IPPs were required to provide for emergency backup power supply, which they had to source from the incumbents at very high cost. Second, the incumbents largely refrained from competing for each other's customers, focusing instead on the small IPPs, but they took the threat seriously and cut both capital expenditure and operating costs to increase competitiveness. Finally, skyrocketing oil prices have put the IPPs at a disadvantage since most of them are more reliant on oil-fired power generation than are the more diversified incumbents.

Paradoxically, the net result of deregulation in the electric power industry has been higher returns for shareholders as incumbents ratcheted up performance only to face unexpectedly weak competition from IPPs. Attracted by the relatively safe revenues and high dividend yields of the incumbents, investors bid up share prices, enabling most of Japan's major electric power companies to deliver TRS of between 5 and 15 percent a year between 1999 and 2005.

Consumer goods companies: Battling a headwind
No consumer goods manufacturers made it into our sample of 57 Japanese companies (they were all too small – an interesting fact in itself). Even so, this is an important sector, and one of those most directly affected by the market forces we have been describing. As a result, it is facing an era of fundamental change and restructuring.

Consumer goods manufacturers in Japan, like those in high tech, face a stagnant and overcrowded market. In personal care products and packaged goods, for instance, the market was essentially flat between 1995 and 2000, while alcohol consumption actually fell by 1 percent a year.[15] Exacerbating this lack of growth is the proliferation of players and excessive competition in most product areas. Japan has four major beer manufacturers, eight major manufacturers of women's hair products, and over 1,400 soy sauce breweries.[16]

To develop a granular perspective on what is changing in the consumer products industry and how the manufacturers are coping, we examined several of the leading players using our granular growth decomposition database. We found that successful companies are compensating for the stagnant and cut-throat domestic market by carrying out significant M&A both at home and abroad, and by pursuing aggressive growth strategies outside Japan.

Kirin, Japan's most venerable beer manufacturer, was able to achieve 2 percent revenue growth between 1999 and 2005, though this came from outside its core domestic business, which actually declined by about 1 percent a year. Market shrinkage and share loss cost the company ¥170 billion in revenues, but it countered by acquiring a 45 percent stake in New Zealand's Lion Nathan in 2000 and Seagram's Four Roses Brand in 2001, adding ¥122 billion in revenues.[17] The company used M&A not only to compensate for the poor performance of its home market but to diversify its domestic portfolio and build a base for growth overseas.

Kirin has continued to grow and diversify its portfolio, most recently by making a friendly bid to acquire a little over 50 percent of Mercian, a leading wine producer, importer, and distributor, for ¥24.7 billion, thereby adding ¥99.5 billion in sales to its portfolio as of 2006.

Most of Kirin's organic growth in this period came from its soft drinks business, which has grown at 5 percent CAGR through a combination of market growth and share gain, adding ¥100 billion in revenues. Kirin also used M&A to extend its portfolio of businesses to the fast-growing pharmaceutical arena, adding ¥50 billion in revenues by acquiring pharmaceutical and biotech companies such as French seed-potato cultivator Germicopa, in which it bought a 71 percent stake in 2001.

Kirin's acquisitions, particularly Lion Nathan, have reshaped its portfolio and growth toward the Asia-Pacific region, which contributed almost ¥160 billion in revenues during this period, producing an annualized growth rate of almost 200 percent (two-thirds of which was inorganic). The region now comprises 10 percent of Kirin's overall revenues and accounts for more than 95 percent of its overall growth.

Kao, Japan's leading consumer products and personal care manufacturer, grew at 2.3 percent a year between 1999 and 2005. Revenues in its core consumer products business grew by 2 percent (CAGR) and in its prestige cosmetics business by 3 percent. Once again, a granular view shows that only 0.6 percent of this growth came from organic growth; almost three times as much (1.7 percent) came from M&A, primarily in overseas markets.

Kao achieved organic growth of only 0.2 percent in the consumer products business during this period, suffering significant market share losses (of ¥23 billion in sales) and relatively slow growth in the underlying market (adding ¥33 billion in sales). It compensated for this lack of organic growth by adding ¥64 billion in revenues from acquisitions in North America and Europe. The largest was the US$450 million acquisition of US-based John Frieda Professional Hair Care in 2002.

Kao also struggled to grow its prestige cosmetics business organically between 1999 and 2005, when share losses amounting to ¥25.5 billion more than cancelled out a ¥21 billion increase in sales from underlying market growth. To boost growth, Kao acquired UK-based Molton Brown from the private-equity firm Bridgepoint for £170 million in 2005, adding ¥20 billion in overseas revenues.

From a geographic perspective, the breakdown of Kao's growth is striking. While the company managed to eke out a mere 0.4 percent a year growth at home (all organic) and 3.9 percent growth in Asia-Pacific (largely organic), it grew by over 10 percent a year in North America and Europe, primarily through M&A. As of 2005, 69 percent of its revenues came from Japan, 20 percent from North America and Europe, and 11 percent from Asia-Pacific.

Survival of the fittest
Increasingly challenging market conditions, coupled with fundamental changes in the nature of Japanese capitalism, are going to accelerate the evolutionary shakeout already under way here.

Consumers get fewer and older
The Japanese population began to decline in 2005, and with fertility rates falling below 1.3 children per woman, this trend is expected to continue for the foreseeable future as the population shrinks from 127 million in 2005 to a projected 90 million in 2055 (Figure 5.8). The country will age too, with huge implications for consumption patterns. The biggest consumers, those aged 35 to 59, will fall from 35 percent of the population to just 28 percent, while the much more abstemious 70-plus segment will grow from 12 percent in 2005 to 33 percent in 2055.[18] Japanese companies already struggling with intense competition in their home market will face a double whammy as the population shrinks, ages, and consumes less.

5.8 Demographic and consumption trends
2005–55 (Forecast)

Population Thousands				CAGR Percent	Average monthly consumption per household[†] ¥, 2003
126,697*					
70~	14,899	115,224		1.4	217,776
60–69	14,842	29,337	89,930	−0.4	274,033
50–59	19,176			−1.0	345,292
		15,517	30,315		
35–49	24,831	17,404		−1.1	305,922
			12,040		
25–34	18,567	20,268	11,682	−1.7	235,119
15–24	15,910	12,069	13,986	−1.7	168,405[‡]
		9,479	7,831		
0–14	18,472	11,150	6,559 7,516	−1.8	N/A
	2005	2030	2055		

* Excluding people whose ages are not available
† Based on the age of household head
‡ Average monthly consumption of households whose heads are less than 25 years old
Source: National Institute of Population and Social Security Research, 2006; National survey of family income and expenditure, 2003; McKinsey analysis

Shareholders get more demanding

Or perhaps we should say a triple whammy, since companies also have to come to terms with increasingly demanding shareholders. Sophisticated, value-oriented shareholders are acquiring larger stakes in Japan and Japanese companies. The cross-shareholding relationships that have locked in business relationships and protected stakeholders at the expense of shareholders are unwinding rapidly. The proportion of shares held in this way fell from 17.1 percent in 1996 to just under 7.6 percent in 2003, while the proportion held by so-called "stable" shareholders fell from 43.4 to 24.3 percent of the overall market over the same period.[19] Foreign institutions and individuals, who tend to be more value-oriented and aggressive, have increased their stake in the Japanese stock market from 12 to 22 percent (Figure 5.9).[20] As of 2007, foreign ownership has reached 28 percent of total market capitalization in Japan and is still growing.[21]

5.9 Shareholding patterns in Japan

Percent of total market capitalization

☐ Stable shareholdings
▨ Cross-holdings
■ Shares held by foreigners

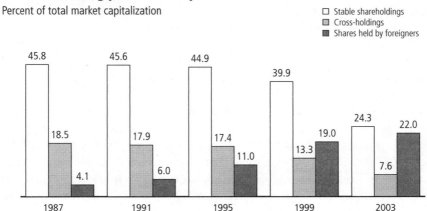

Source: Nissei Life Insurance Research Institute; Tokyo Stock Exchange

Shareholders of Japanese companies are already becoming more assertive, and will continue to do so. Foreign activist funds in particular are launching more frequent shareholder motions (something that anyone who holds at least 1 percent of the shares in a listed company can do). Forty such motions are expected to be filed in 2007, twice the annual average for the past decade. To date, most have focused on increasing dividends, but some recent examples have concerned a broader range of issues including the removal or appointment of directors and the dismantling of "poison pill" defenses against takeover.[22]

Proxy fights with recalcitrant shareholders have also become a reality for Japanese management following the dramatic victory of upstart Ichigo Asset Management in blocking the management-supported sale of Tokyo Kohtetsu to Nippon Steel-owned Osaka Steel in February 2007. Ichigo held a 10.96 percent stake in Tokyo Kohtetsu and opposed the sale on the grounds that the exchange ratio, which provided an acquisition premium of only 0.3 percent, was unfair to Tokyo Kohtetsu's shareholders and fell far short of the average 30 percent acquisition premium of recent buyouts in Japan. Osaka Steel refused to raise the exchange ratio and Tokyo Kohtetsu's management supported the sale, following advice from Nikko Cordial and Mitsubishi UFJ securities and backing from the Mitsui group. In response, Ichigo launched a proxy campaign, collecting 33 percent of Tokyo Kohtetsu's voting rights (with proxies for 16 percent of the voting rights from 500 individual shareholders and 7 percent from institutions). At an extraordinary shareholders' meeting on 22 February 2007, Ichigo was able to block the two-thirds majority that management needed to gain approval for the sale.[23]

Such assertive shareholder behavior serves to underline the changing nature of the relationship between management and shareholders. But activist shareholders won't always get their own way when they seek to assert their ownership role over other stakeholders. Conservative forces within Japan's political, business, and judicial circles have already begun to strike back. By mid-2007, more than 300 Japanese companies had introduced rights plans and other poison-pill provisions, and the courts have upheld the validity of these provisions and deemed them applicable to a broad range of activist measures.[24] During the June 2007 cycle of shareholder meetings, every single activist proposal was defeated, often by individual Japanese shareholders overwhelmingly supporting management against foreign activists. In addition, the Tokyo District Court recently handed out a two-year jail sentence to Yoshiaki Murakami, a well-known activist, on conviction for insider trading. It applied a very broad definition of insider trading that seemed intended to inhibit activist shareholders' ability to make specific proposals to company management.[25]

Despite this recent backlash, though, the overall trend is undoubtedly toward more informed and active shareholder behavior.

M&A gets more popular

In the past, M&A has played a much smaller role in shaping the economy in Japan than in other developed countries, but this is changing. The number and size of transactions has soared from 351 with a total value of ¥1 trillion in 1996 to 2,309 with a total value of ¥10 trillion in 2005.[26] Foreigners are already active, accounting for 179 transactions in 2005, and the introduction in 2007 of new regulations allowing triangular stock mergers[27] is expected to boost the number and size of acquisitions by overseas buyers. Though rare, hostile bids, previously unheard of in Japan, are now becoming acceptable: an all-time high of four were launched in 2006.[28]

While most takeovers continue to be friendly and most hostile bids still come from foreign activists (particularly the Steel Partners fund), 2006 saw a bid by a Japanese strategic buyer that was acknowledged to be hostile (Oji Paper's failed bid to acquire competitor Hokuetsu) and a friendly but unwelcome bid by leading menswear maker Aoki to acquire competitor Futata (which also failed when Futata chose to sell to white knight Konaka).[29] Private-equity buyers have also emerged as a force to be reckoned with in Japan: several high-profile deals have already gone through and billions of dollars are earmarked for Japan. Teams of professionals from most of the major global (and domestic) private-equity firms are now scouring the country for deals.

The way forward

For too long, Japanese companies have been onlookers at the global M&A dance. This must change if companies and the overall economy are to continue to prosper. Companies in high tech, consumer goods, retail, and a host of other sectors will have to take a more active approach to both domestic consolidation and globalization, and rely more heavily on M&A to do so.

Given the mixed results Japanese companies have had with M&A in the past, they will need to adopt new skills and new models. Private-equity players will set new precedents and in some cases even provide cover for the fundamental restructuring of domestic acquisitions.

A few companies such as Asahi Glass have already pioneered new models for integrating and leveraging the management teams of their foreign acquisitions. Asahi is the world's leading glass manufacturer, and its approach to global M&A may have relevance for many Japanese companies. Having acquired control of the venerable Belgian glass manufacturer Glaverbel in 1981, Asahi found that its management team had the capabilities and experience to lead global M&A for the group. Since then, the Glaverbel team has taken the initiative not only in identifying and capturing M&A opportunities at the global level but also in carrying out the post-acquisition integration and restructuring needed to realize synergies.

For its part, Asahi provides overall direction, supplies funding, and takes the lead in working with acquired companies to achieve long-term performance improvement. Between 1999 and 2005, Asahi Glass grew at 3.5 percent a year and generated annual TRS of 10 percent. It has built a geographically diversified business portfolio with 45 percent of revenues coming from Japan, 21 percent from Asia, 21 percent from Europe, and 13 percent from the Americas in 2005.

In 2006, Nihon Sheet Glass, Asahi's major domestic rival, took a leaf out of Asahi's book by acquiring the UK's Pilkington for £1.8 billion. Founded in 1826, Pilkington invented the modern float-glass manufacturing process. With £2.4 billion in sales and 24,000 employees, it was twice the size of

NSG, which then had sales of ¥265 billion and 12,000 employees. The combined company has operations in 27 countries and a global market share of 15 percent, close behind Asahi, making it the world's number two glass manufacturer. NSG has positioned the seasoned Pilkington management team to lead the development and execution of the group's global growth strategy.

■ ■ ■

The global economy is changing quickly, and with it the nature of Japanese capitalism. The companies that adopt a mindset that is more aggressive, driven by shareholder value, and receptive to M&A as a useful tool for tackling domestic consolidation and globalization alike will be able to make the right granular choices to grow. Those that don't are likely to go – and probably sooner than they think.

NOTES

1   WMM.

2   Tokyo Stock Exchange, 1st section.

3   TSE.

4   *Annual Report on National Accounts* (2005).

5   Indexed to 1995.

6   The restructuring of some of the most problematic companies (more than 40 in total) was channelled through the Industrial Revitalization Corporation of Japan (IRCJ), the "good bank/bad bank" workout vehicle established by the government to facilitate financial and operational cleanup between the government, management, shareholders, and lenders.

7   Ministry of Finance.

8   *Denki Sangyo Handbook.*

9   Gartner/Dataquest, RIC.

10 World Fab Watch Database 2007.

11 *Nikkei Shinbun*, June 2, 2006.

12 World Fab Watch Database 2007.

13 Research Insight; annual reports.

14 *Denki Shinbun, Nikkei Shinbun.*

15 Annual Statistics for Cosmetic Products; Nikkan Keizai; National Tax Agency.

16 Nikkan Keizai; Japan Soy Sauce Brewers' Association.

17 Kirin annual reports; press releases; company website.

18 National Survey of Family Income and Expenditure, 2003.

19 Nissei Life Insurance Research Institute.

20 TSE.

21 TSE.

22 *Nikkei Shinbun; Shoji Homu.*

23 *International Financial Law Review, Japan Times, Financial Times.*

24 In July 2007 the Tokyo High Court ruled that a rights plan introduced by Bull-Dog Sauce Co. Ltd to fend off a hostile takeover bid by US hedge fund Steel Partners did not violate the principle of shareholder equality, and branded Steel as an "abusive acquirer."

25 In effect, the court found that information becomes subject to provisions against insider trading as soon as a company begins to consider it, rather than at the point where it is incorporated into the company's strategy and business plans.

26 *Nikkei Shinbun.*

27 Transactions in which a foreign company with a Japanese subsidiary can now acquire a Japanese company by having it merge with the acquirer's local subsidiary using the shares of the acquiring parent as consideration for the shareholders of the target company.

28 *Nikkei Shinbun.*

29 *Nikkei Shinbun; Japan Times; Konaka IR.*

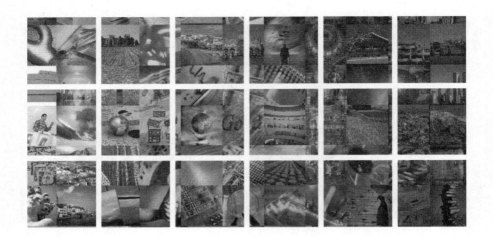

6

Opportunities for growth and innovation in Southeast Asia

Jonathan Auerbach and Carl Harris

IT'S NOW TEN YEARS SINCE the Asian currency crisis and the smoke from Indonesian fires first cast a crippling haze – metaphorical and literal – across Southeast Asia. Since then, China and India have hogged the headlines as the prime movers of Asia's global resurgence. Multinationals have quickly developed perspectives on how to participate in these markets, realizing that not to do so puts them at risk of global irrelevance.

Overlooked in the clamor of the debate about Asia's future are those economies once acclaimed as the region's tigers. Yet these markets have quietly been re-establishing stability and rapid growth – not as before on the back of a surge of capital and other factor inputs, but rather on a foundation of productivity improvements and supply chains with links into China, India, and Japan. With its compelling combination of rising middle-class incomes, economic liberalization, new investor mindset, and mounting intra-Asian trade, all underpinned by valuable natural resources, Southeast Asia is becoming a growth engine again. Yet many multinational companies are failing to pay it the attention it deserves.

Southeast Asia represents a huge market of 568 million people, with GDP growth running at between 5.5 and 6 percent and a GDP per capita of US$1,825.[1] What's more, low labor costs in countries such as Indonesia, the Philippines, and Vietnam make these countries a genuine alternative to China in manufacturing or India in business-process outsourcing.

Let's begin our assessment of the opportunities for growth in Southeast Asia by taking a clear-eyed look at the issues that have historically impeded the development of the region, as several of these issues also open up attractive growth opportunities for the companies that take the time to understand them.

Challenges for foreign investors

Once the darling of foreign investors, Southeast Asia's markets are now more likely to be described – in the foreign press at least – as fragmented and complex, weak in their investment climates and lacking in both key infrastructure and stability. There is some truth in this, but it is not the whole story. Fragmented it may be, but the region is also growing rapidly and presents real opportunities for innovation.

Fragmented markets

Southeast Asia's economies vary widely in their level of development and rates of growth. They fall naturally into three groups: middle-income countries, emerging economies, and Singapore.

Middle-income countries. Forming the bulk of Southeast Asia and accounting for more than three-quarters of the GDP of the ASEAN[2] grouping are the four middle-income countries of Indonesia, Malaysia, the Philippines, and Thailand. The small sultanate of Brunei also fits into this category.

Emerging economies. Since 2002, Vietnam, Laos, and Cambodia have enjoyed double-digit growth and made good progress in alleviating poverty, but their economies start from a low GDP base. As their leaders develop experience in reforming their economies, they are increasingly engaging with the international community in meeting global economic norms. After nearly a decade of negotiations, Vietnam became a full member of the World Trade Organization in January 2007.

Singapore. This city-state has a high GDP per capita and has generated significant wealth by investing ahead of growth. With a GDP per capita that ranks twenty-eighth in the world,[3] Singapore has leveraged its strategic location to produce a nimble growth-oriented economy that balances high-value manufacturing with services.

Concentrated ownership

In many segments of these economies, ownership tends to be closely held by family groups or state-owned enterprises (SOEs). Some are unlisted or heavily consolidated, reducing transparency and making it harder for outsiders to see broader market opportunities.

Before the region's local stock exchanges were established,[4] corporate capital was raised largely from family-owned conglomerates and the state. In 1999, a World Bank analysis estimated that the ten leading families in Thailand, Indonesia, and the Philippines controlled half of each country's corporate sector by market capitalization. Family groups remain important: in the Philippines, the four listed Ayala companies (Globe, BPI, Ayala Corp., and ALI) still account for roughly a third of the market capitalization of the Philippine Stock Exchange composite index.[5]

Even in the global financial center of Singapore, the state's investment companies continue to control more than a fifth of the market capitalization of the local stock exchange. Similarly, in Malaysia the state and its holding companies control roughly a third of the market capitalization of the Bursa Malaysia. And then there are the unlisted SOE giants such as Malaysia's Petronas and Indonesia's Pertamina, both of which figure in the top 10 of the *Financial Times'* global "Non-public 150" list.

Things are changing, however. Consider Vietnam, where the government has consolidated the number of SOEs from around 19,000 to 2,500 since the mid-1990s. Even so, they still represent around 10 percent of the country's employment and 20 percent of its domestic investment, and contribute 40 percent to its budget. A new state capital investment corporation is attempting to rationalize the state-owned sector further through privatization and consolidation, with the aim of reducing the number of SOEs to around 1,500 in the next four years.

On the whole, governments in Southeast Asia have viewed state ownership not as a hindrance to wealth creation but as an important tool for economic development.

Market size
It's true that China and India are larger than Southeast Asia and have grown faster over the past decade. It's hardly surprising that their populations of more than a billion each and China's headline-grabbing 12 percent annual growth should have attracted investors' attention. Yet investors shouldn't overlook the fact that Southeast Asia's markets collectively offer a population of almost 600 million. Nor should we forget that India and China themselves are not homogenous opportunities, composed as they are of multiple provinces with different languages, ethnic mixes, regulations, and consumer habits.

Lack of infrastructure
The lack of infrastructure in key sectors in developing economies can present a real obstacle to doing business. Some Southeast Asian countries have banking systems that are still not fully configured to serve lower-income segments, especially when it comes to micro-payments. Distribution systems are often undeveloped, and the region as a whole, with the notable exception of Singapore, suffers from a limited fixed-line telecommunications network. In addition, the "soft" intermediary businesses and enablers that lower barriers to entry in the West – small-business banking, executive recruitment, competitive open access to retail channels, and the like – tend to be less developed.

Political instability
Although many of the countries of Southeast Asia have adopted more stable political frameworks, some investors' perceptions are still colored by such events as Thailand's 2006 coup and the Bali bombings. There are no easy answers, and the region's politics are beyond our remit here. But it is fair to

say that the economic benefits of political and social stability are clear to the region's growing middle class.

Where the opportunities lie

To dwell on the challenges of operating in this region is to risk neglecting the real business opportunities it presents. Indeed, many of the issues we've just described open up attractive growth opportunities for companies that take the trouble to understand them and then move quickly. Although the fragmented nature of these markets can be frustrating, for instance, it may mean there is less risk of attack from outside. Relatively closed markets bring higher margins for those that understand them. Because global companies have yet to pay much attention to the region, there are unique opportunities for innovation and areas where margins are attractive.

Similarly, Southeast Asia's markets may be smaller, but its profit pools are less contested, leaving significant value to be captured. In credit cards, for instance, we estimate that the average margin in 2005 across Southeast Asia was 23 percent, considerably higher than China's 16 percent and not far off India's 29 percent. These market effects are even more stark when we look at revenue pools:[6] the 2005 revenue pool for credit cards in Southeast Asia was an estimated US$627 million, compared to US$440 million in India and a mere US$159 million in China.

Tailwinds in consumer markets

Many of the region's sub-sectors are growing furiously. The rapidly expanding middle class is driving rapid growth in consumer markets, many of which are close to setting off along their S-curves and catching new tailwinds. Provided they are approached properly, these growth opportunities can yield dramatic results.

In the 1990s, Philippine fast-food company Jollibee sought to benefit from the tailwind of a segment that was growing at between 15 and 20 percent a year.[7] With its offer to consumers of "great taste and happiness," Jollibee built a brand tailored to local preferences. Thanks to a clear understanding of the region's consumer market and excellent operational abilities, it left international rivals standing.

The capital injection resulting from its 1993 listing on the Manila stock market enabled Jollibee to use acquisitions to move into other segments. In 1994 it acquired a Philippine chain of 50 pizza outlets, doubled their revenues within a year, and went on to open 50 more outlets over the next three years.

6.1 Jollibee's international expansion

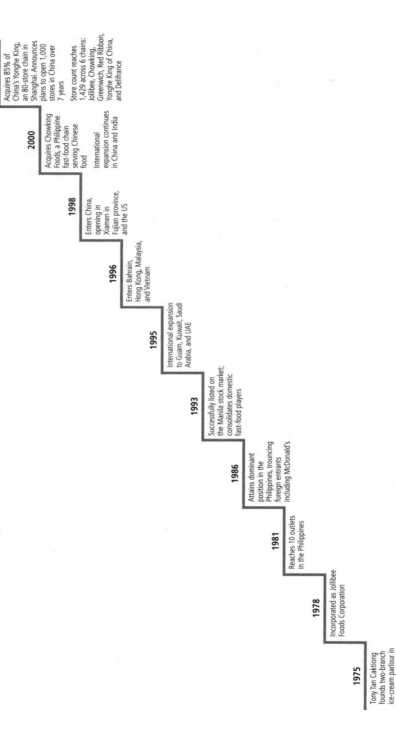

1975
Tony Tan Caktiong founds two-branch ice-cream parlour in Manila selling Philippine sandwiches and hamburgers

1978
Incorporated as Jollibee Foods Corporation

1981
Reaches 10 outlets in the Philippines

1986
Attains dominant position in the Philippines, trouncing foreign entrants including McDonald's

1993
Successfully listed on the Manila stock market; consolidates domestic fast-food players

1995
International expansion to Guam, Kuwait, Saudi Arabia, and UAE

1996
Enters Bahrain, Hong Kong, Malaysia, and Vietnam

1998
Enters China, opening in Xiamen in Fujian province, and the US

2000
Acquires Chowking Foods, a Philippine fast-food chain serving Chinese food

International expansion continues in China and India

2006
Acquires 85% of China's Yonghe King, an 80-store chain in Shanghai. Announces plans to open 1,000 stores in China over 7 years

Store count reaches 1,429 across 6 chains: Jollibee, Chowking, Greenwich, Red Ribbon, Yonghe King of China, and Delifrance

Source: Press articles

Jollibee then invested in a local chain of Chinese food takeaway outlets. In the late 1990s, having expanded across multiple segments in the Philippines, Jollibee took its flagship brand global. It set up operations in areas with large Filipino expatriate communities in the Gulf, Taiwan, and the US, but with mixed success.

More recent moves show that Jollibee is now focused on finding fresh tailwinds of consumer spending in new markets that offer prospects like those in the Philippines. In 2006 it acquired 85 percent of a large fast-food chain in China, YongHe King, with some 80 stores in Shanghai, Beijing, Shenzhen, Wuhan, Hangzhou, and other cities. Jollibee's challenge will be to replicate in this new environment the growth strategy that served it so well in its home market (Figure 6.1).

Financial services is another sector where companies have grown by riding tailwinds of consumer spending. In Malaysia, Public Bank has benefited from riding a tailwind in consumer growth, as well as in serving small and medium-sized enterprises. Founded by its current chairman in 1966, Public Bank is

6.2 Growth in consumer loans

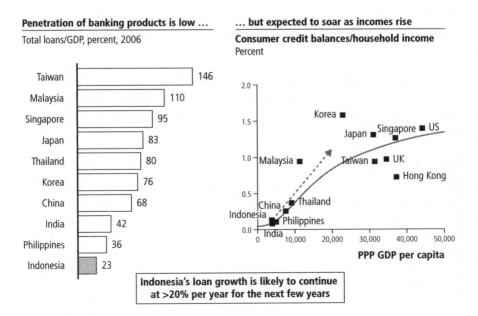

Penetration of banking products is low ...

Total loans/GDP, percent, 2006

Taiwan	146
Malaysia	110
Singapore	95
Japan	83
Thailand	80
Korea	76
China	68
India	42
Philippines	36
Indonesia	23

... but expected to soar as incomes rise

Consumer credit balances/household income
Percent

PPP GDP per capita

Indonesia's loan growth is likely to continue at >20% per year for the next few years

Source: EIU; Global Insight; McKinsey analysis

the third-largest bank in the country. It leveraged its fast-growing consumer business to sustain double-digit revenue growth across two business cycles from 1992 to 2005. Between 1999 and 2005 it delivered an average total return to shareholders of 18 percent and saw its market capitalization grow from US$385 million to US$5.7 billion. It has also been quick to move into new businesses such as Islamic finance in the home market.

If we look ahead, Indonesia and the Philippines seem poised for dispro-portionate growth in personal financial services over the next few years. Vietnam is looking forward to annual growth of 16 percent in revenues over the next decade, while Indonesia is benefiting from its position on the S-curve and enjoying growth of roughly 20 percent a year (Figure 6.2).

Getting the right business model

Before companies can serve the emerging base of aspirant consumers in these markets, they must carefully configure their business models. They need consumer value propositions to attract low-income customers and implement lean operations that make it possible to reap viable margins. In essence, companies in Southeast Asia are finding profits earlier in the S-curve and shifting it in their favor by getting growth sooner in lower-income consumer segments. These innovative business models have to strike the right balance between keeping their cost to serve low and offering customers a sufficiently extensive initial product or service range. That way, companies can increase market size while keeping products (and profits) attractive.

A multitude of companies are managing to do this well. Two of them are Indonesia's Telkomsel, which innovated to produce affordable cellphone services, and Manila Water in the Philippines, which pioneered community billing to turn around its utility business.

The leading cellphone operator in Indonesia, Telkomsel illustrates that though global cellphone technologies are broadly similar, there are spectacular differences in the profitability of individual providers. This variability derives from a combination of factors including the level of competition, the maturity of the market, and the fine-tuning of business models to local market conditions. Thus, while the European average EBITDA[8] among GSM operators is around 35 percent, Telkomsel's model delivers an impressive 72 percent. Moreover, it does so on an average revenue of roughly US$9 per subscriber per month, compared to the European average of US$40.

How does Telkomsel achieve this? Having a high market share – 56 percent of the home market – obviously helps. Given its dependence on network economics, cellular telecom is broadly a fixed-cost business. Even so, many European operators achieve much lower profitability while using the same technology from the same vendors and having a market share in the same range. Vodafone, for instance, has 47 percent market share in Ireland and an EBITDA of 45 percent; similarly, Telefonica has a 46 percent market share in Spain and an EBITDA of 45 percent.

The secret of Telkomsel's success lies in the steps it has taken to meet local needs profitably. First, it designed pricing packages suitable for all the various income groups in Indonesia, so as to expand its potential market. As a result, prepaid customers, who comprise 87 percent of the customer base, buy a fixed amount of call time sold in very small units (typically at less than US$1 per top-up).

Second, Telkomsel has been innovative in driving down its costs in selling to and serving low-revenue customers. To reduce selling costs, it employs local representatives who sell minutes using their own cellphones equipped with special SIM cards. Its distribution network consists of hundred of thousands of representatives from a broad range of Indonesia's urban and rural populations: shopkeepers, housewives, street vendors, and others. By forsaking traditional retail channels in favor of its own network, Telkomsel has built up an extremely loyal sales force and created a significant first-mover advantage.

Access to a low-cost reliable water supply makes an enormous difference to the quality of life in poor communities. In the Philippines, Manila Water was able to bring low-income customers into its system by introducing community-based billing. It mobilized local entrepreneurs by employing some 10,000 contractors and couriers as agents. This proved a winning strategy and a profitable one, yielding an ROIC of 19 percent per year over the three years to 2006.

Acquiring to grow across borders

The superficial differences among the markets of Southeast Asia often mask the features they share in common. A consumer in Bangkok resembles a consumer in Jakarta more closely, in terms of profile and needs, than one in Mukdaharn or any of the other smaller cities of northern Thailand. Our research indicates that such resemblances grow closer as consumers become more affluent. As a result, a business model that does well in one market in

Southeast Asia has a good chance of being successful in others. A company entering the region with a clear portfolio logic can often cascade this growth across multiple markets.

Companies with insights into how these consumer markets are growing have been able to position themselves for strong regional growth before the growth potential has been embedded in acquisition prices. Singapore's telecom company SingTel is one player that has capitalized on its deep local market knowledge and an inorganic growth strategy.

SingTel has leveraged a home-base advantage in Southeast Asia to achieve growth through M&A in other markets, as recorded in many business cases.[9]

6.3 SingTel's regional expansion

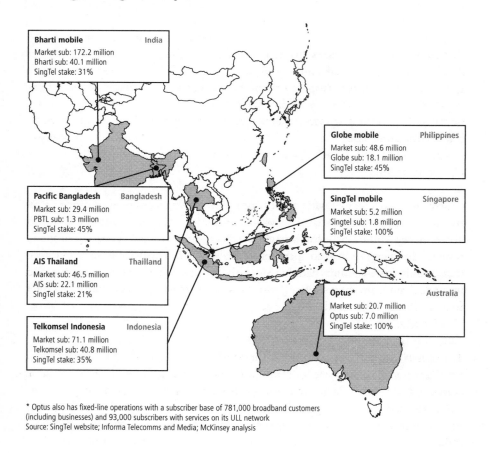

Bharti mobile   India
Market sub: 172.2 million
Bharti sub: 40.1 million
SingTel stake: 31%

Globe mobile   Philippines
Market sub: 48.6 million
Globe sub: 18.1 million
SingTel stake: 45%

Pacific Bangladesh   Bangladesh
Market sub: 29.4 million
PBTL sub: 1.3 million
SingTel stake: 45%

SingTel mobile   Singapore
Market sub: 5.2 million
Singtel sub: 1.8 million
SingTel stake: 100%

AIS Thailand   Thailand
Market sub: 46.5 million
AIS sub: 22.1 million
SingTel stake: 21%

Optus*   Australia
Market sub: 20.7 million
Optus sub: 7.0 million
SingTel stake: 100%

Telkomsel Indonesia   Indonesia
Market sub: 71.1 million
Telkomsel sub: 40.8 million
SingTel stake: 35%

* Optus also has fixed-line operations with a subscriber base of 781,000 broadband customers (including businesses) and 93,000 subscribers with services on its ULL network
Source: SingTel website; Informa Telecomms and Media; McKinsey analysis

In the mid-1990s, it embarked on a regional program of growth through inorganic expansion. This has resulted in significant stakes in seven fixed-line and cellphone operators in the region to date. Thanks to this strategy, the company's revenues have grown from S$4.9 billion in 2000 to S$13.0 billion in 2006, while its EBITDA has risen from S$3.0 billion to S$6.7 billion (Figure 6.3).

According to analyst estimates, roughly 77 percent of the SingTel Group's value now derives from its international holdings.[10] And while not all of its investments have proved successful, it's hard to argue with the overall results. During this expansion period, acquisitions delivered a cumulative internal rate of return of 19 percent, generated value in excess of S$30 billion, and lifted investments from their original value of S$19.7 billion to an estimated S$50 billion today.[11] SingTel has created this value by leveraging the cash generated at its home base to make bold investments in operators in other markets to which it believes it can bring distinctive insight.

Capturing white spaces of opportunity

High growth in less developed markets in Southeast Asia opens up white spaces of opportunity, especially in infrastructure and distribution, along what is an increasingly complex value chain. When these white spaces are addressed with the disruptive technological innovations, there is real scope to build large franchises.

PLDT-Smart is a leading cellular telecom player in the Philippines that has developed a unique and virtually cost-free transaction and billing system called SmartMoney. This is a fast, over-the-air, real-time system that is able to handle the hundreds of millions of top-ups and transactions needed to serve its predominantly low-income customer base. Over time, the company refined this capability to provide a reliable payments service between individuals called Smart Padala. Since the Philippines lacked accessible and inexpensive remittance services, the business grew rapidly and now has over five million registered users generating aggregate revenues of over US$8 million a day.

Though it started out with an investment in telecom, PLDT now owns a leading global architecture for small-scale payment transactions. So distinctive is its capability that the company has moved into joint ventures in the Middle East, formed a partnership with MTC Vodafone,[12] developed a global partnership with MasterCard, and been emulated by operators in Africa and India.

One interesting feature of Southeast Asian markets is that because many industry structures are unlike those in the west, competition is likely to evolve along a different path. In Malaysia, Indonesia, and Cambodia, for example, a number of players are building broadband internet services businesses, often wireless, with the intention of leapfrogging fixed-line incumbents. Such models have proved more successful here than elsewhere in the world because of the inadequacy of the region's fixed-line infrastructure.

Another interesting example of a company taking advantage of a white space in the market with new technology is Telkomsel in Indonesia in the music industry. Because CD piracy is rife in Indonesia, Telkomsel was able to leverage its market position, trusted brand, and its secure payment system to create the largest music distribution business in the country. Telkomsel has largely been able to protect its music revenues from piracy, turning what many see as a weakness of the market to its advantage. Operating in the same segment as Apple in the US, Telkomsel has used the comparatively greater white space of the Indonesian market to generate millions in revenue a year, while moving up the value chain to the extent that it is now starting to sign artists.

Profiting from market restructuring and regionalization

Another change that companies can turn to their advantage is governments' efforts to introduce an investor mindset into their holding companies. Southeast Asian government-linked companies (GLCs) are becoming more disciplined and market oriented, placing more emphasis on growth and value and opening up opportunities for industry restructuring.

The consolidation of the banking sector in the wake of the Asian financial crisis in 1997 is one clear example. Following the crisis, several Southeast Asian governments mandated the restructuring of their banking sectors. Significant consolidation has followed in some countries, with a view to creating more efficient local players and regional champions.[13]

The ASEAN nations are planning to create a single market by 2015. This deadline is already having an impact in some markets, giving players that have established a strong position an advantage, and those that haven't yet begun the journey an incentive to join in.

Toyota illustrates how a company can shape a regional approach. The Japanese auto manufacturer entered Southeast Asia early via a series of small and relatively inefficient operations built up behind national tariff barriers, a move that allowed it to shape some local markets and develop products tailored to local conditions. In Indonesia, for example, the Toyota Kijang, a rugged, flexible, and capacious utility vehicle, has become the default choice of car for many households.

The creation of the ASEAN Free Trade Area gave Toyota the opportunity to rationalize its operations, cut its costs, and build its regional production volumes to globally efficient levels. While there is insufficient publicly available data for us to examine the company's performance in Southeast Asia specifically, the number of vehicles it sold in Asia outside Japan, China, and Hong Kong has grown fivefold over the past four years. A further indication of Toyota's success is its substantial share of the passenger vehicle market: approximately 40 percent in Thailand, the Philippines, and Indonesia. Shortly after opening its third Thai plant in Ban Pho outside Bangkok in 2007, Toyota announced that it intended to double the plant's output to 200,000 units, mostly for export, taking production in Thailand to more than 650,000 units.

Regional reforms are likely to have a substantial impact on other sectors too. The liberalization of the airline industry – ASEAN has committed to implement an open skies agreement by 2008 – will drive liberalization and strong growth in air travel. Because only local ASEAN companies can legally benefit from this agreement, international airlines have been jockeying to form partnerships with them so as to gain from the expected growth.

Organizing for growth

How can companies organize to grow in the region? There are two clear options: to ride the tailwinds of growth in individual markets, or to gain scale by expanding regionally either organically or through M&A.

Riding tailwinds in individual markets

Some sectors grow much faster than others because of strong tailwinds. Prominent examples are the goods and services sectors driven by Southeast Asia's new consumers, particularly those in the aspirant or lower middle-class segment. Indonesia's growth giants, for example, are consumer goods companies in the fast-food, dairy, cosmetics, and tobacco businesses.

Companies may wish to focus on identifying and exploiting these tailwinds by focusing their activities at a granular level and building business models that respond to the particular challenges of individual local markets.

Motorola's handset business demonstrates what can be achieved by focusing on Southeast Asia. The company identified the opportunity in 2003: "Before, attention given to the China and India market had in a way overshadowed the rest of Asia. This has now changed."[14] Over the next two years, Motorola was able to achieve a 40 percent year-on-year increase in sales in the region, and it now commands a significant share in many of the individual markets (with 22 percent of the market in Vietnam, for instance).[15]

As well as locating key manufacturing facilities in the region, Motorola used its markets – particularly Singapore – to test new products and concepts before rolling them out across the region and beyond. For example, Service One, a one-stop service center for Motorola's products, was market-tested in Singapore before being incorporated into the company's global service model.

Gaining scale across the region

Growth across the region can be organic or inorganic. One good example of M&A-driven growth is that of SingTel, as we saw earlier. The banking sector has also experienced some cross-border investments as national players try to build scale in the region. But organic growth is also an option.

After early forays into China, Thailand's Siam Cement Group (SCG) made a conscious decision to focus principally on growing organically in the ASEAN region. So it built a pipeline of talent, mobilizing its prestige in Thailand to recruit promising graduates and train them across business lines. The resulting management depth enabled it to expand into Indochina by leveraging its domestic operations and its proximity to and knowledge of neighboring markets. It has continued this growth into the rest of Southeast Asia. More than half its sales (in its chemicals, paper, and building materials businesses as well as cement) now come from its ASEAN neighbors.

■ ■ ■

Now is the time for companies to revisit their plans for Southeast Asia and consider expanding their positions here. The historically fragmented nature of these markets, coupled with a dose of political and financial instability, has conspired to keep the opportunities off global companies' radar screens. However, recent sustained growth in these markets, the increased integration of the region, and enhanced political stability make this the perfect time to pay attention to Southeast Asia again. As regional trade integration increases, strong positions in individual countries within Southeast Asia can only become more valuable.

NOTES

1   2006 estimate for Indonesia, Malaysia, Philippines, Singapore, Thailand, and Vietnam, Economist Intelligence Unit.

2   The Association of Southeast Asian Nations. Though Burma, or Myanmar, is formally an ASEAN member we have not included it in our analysis. East Timor and Papua New Guinea are not members of ASEAN.

3   As of July 2007 at purchasing power parity (IndexMundi).

4   Some stock exchanges are still quite young: Thailand's was established in 1977 and Indonesia's in 1979, for instance.

5   As of 28 May 2003: "Special Report: Anniversary report 2003," *BusinessWorld,* 25 July 2003.

6   The revenue pool is defined as the total of all fee and net interest margin before provisions, including the effect of interest margin differences.

7   "Jollibee Foods going global," Case study ICFAI Business School, IBS Research Centre, Kolkata, 306-424-1.

8   Earnings before interest, taxes, depreciation, and amortization.

9   See, for instance, S. Garg and G. Szulanski, "SingTel: Becoming the best regional communications player," INSEAD, 1 July 2005; S. Chaudhuri and U. Roopa, "SingTel's Growth Strategies," ICFAI, 1 July 2004.

10   The average of various analysts' reports.

11   Analysis of public financial statements of SingTel Group and associated companies, 1993 to present.

12   *Manila Bulletin,* 16 March 2007.

13   The first round of consolidation after the 1997 crisis saw Malaysia reduce the number of its banks from 55 to 10, for instance. Consolidation moves elsewhere also offer scope for new entrants. Foreign players are already participating in Indonesia and looking forward to having greater access to the markets of Thailand, the Philippines and Vietnam.

14   *New Straits Times,* Malaysia, 23 October 2003.

15   *Straits Times,* Singapore, 26 October 2004; *Business Times,* Singapore, 5 March 2005.

7

South Korea: At the crossroads of growth

Wonsik Choi and Sangbeom Kim

NOT SO LONG AGO Korea was one of the fastest-growing economies in the world, a powerhouse that enjoyed decades of GDP growth at 7 or 8 percent or even more. But in the late 1990s, everything changed. As the economy became more developed and felt the effects of the Asian economic crisis and a personal-credit crisis, growth slowed dramatically, to a rate close to the OECD average. The impact on the economy and on Korean corporations was profound, and continues to be felt today.

So what were the causes of the slowdown? The structure of Korea's manufacturing sector is clearly one of them. If we look at exports, all seems well: they have continued to grow at more than 10 percent a year over the past five years, reaching US$320 billion in 2006. But if we turn to imports, the problem is apparent: they have grown just as fast as exports, to reach much the same level of US$310 billion in 2006. Why has this happened?

The fact is that Korea has barely any natural resources of its own, so most of its process manufacturing relies on the import of raw materials such as oil, gas, iron ore, and copper. Korean assembly manufacturers also rely heavily on foreign suppliers – not just for low-cost parts (which they buy mainly from China) but for high-technology components (which they buy mainly from Japan) as well, since they still don't have all the expertise they need to manufacture these components themselves. The upshot is that the more Korea exports, the more it imports.

Another difficulty for Korea is that the competitiveness of its manufacturing sector is undermined by foreign exchange (because of the appreciation of the Korean won), transportation costs (the rising price of oil), and the uncertain labor environment (the inflexibility of unions). At the same time, manufacturers are facing competitive threats from the developed economies of the US, Japan, and Europe, as well as from newly emerging nations such as China and India.

The slackening in the pace of growth of domestic consumption and investment is another factor in Korea's economic slowdown. Household consumption and local investment account for more than half of total GDP. However, their compound annual growth rate (CAGR) has fallen from its historic rate of between 8 and 12 percent a year to 4 or 5 percent over the past five years.

There are several reasons for this drop in domestic growth. When the financial crisis of the late 1990s was followed by a consumer credit-card crisis, Korean companies reacted with extreme caution. They reduced their overall level of investment to concentrate on financial soundness. The debt/equity ratio has improved significantly over the past ten years, while investment ratios have dropped. As a result, Korean companies have recently started to pursue direct investment overseas, rather than investing at home, in the quest for lower-cost manufacturing and local market presence.

The government is working with Korean companies to address these challenges, notably by introducing free trade agreements to help industries become more globally competitive and by maintaining lower interest rates to promote domestic consumption and investment. However, their efforts are being hindered by inflationary pressures created by rising real-estate prices as well as hikes in the cost of crude oil and other imported raw materials. Korea and its companies are now at a crossroads: they must either find an entirely new way to achieve the levels of growth they used to take for granted or resign themselves to low growth for the foreseeable future.

Growth at any cost?

Before the Asian financial crisis, many Korean corporations pursued growth by exploiting debt financing, often at the expense of their profitability and financial stability. Many believed that growth would automatically translate into value creation and thought they would be able to continue raising capital to fund new growth and rolling over their existing debt-financing obligations indefinitely. But the Asian crisis marked a turning-point. Many Korean corp-orations could scarcely summon enough operating profits to cover interest payments, let alone honor lenders' requests to pay back principal. Thrown into financial distress, a large number of them fell prey to bankruptcy. Scale was no defense, as Daewoo Group, formerly the country's second-largest conglomerate, bears witness.

Following the crisis, the government introduced the concept of conglomerates with interlinked liabilities and imposed various regulations on them. Their purpose was to curb unbridled expansion by Korean companies and help maintain their financial soundness, thereby mitigating any risks to the overall economy, which is highly dependent on large conglomerates. For their part, Korean corporations became far more attentive to their profitability and financial soundness – sometimes excessively so, at the cost of slowing their investment in future growth. They have learned the lesson that growth by itself is not sufficient for prosperity (or indeed for survival); rather, it has to create value and be pursued within the limits imposed by a company's financial situation.

If we look at more developed economies such as those of the United States and Australia, we see an interesting picture. Here, focusing on profits to the exclusion of growth in the longer term correlates strongly with poor total returns to shareholders (TRS) and often spells corporate extinction.[1] A ten-year analysis of companies reveals that low-growth companies were six times more likely to "die" or be acquired than high-growth ones, as well as turning in a TRS performance 25 percent lower than that of high-growth companies.

To look at the situation faced by Korean companies, we took the 60 largest listed companies in terms of market capitalization and revenue in 1993[2] and tracked their financial performance across two business cycles, from 1993 to 1998 and from 1998 to 2005. For the purpose of our analysis, we classified companies as high-growth if they achieved a rate of revenue growth above the rate of Korean GDP growth in the first cycle. In the first cycle, there were 39 high-growth and 21 low-growth companies. In the second cycle, we identified 27 high-growth and 24 low-growth companies.[3] We then looked at the relevance of growth to the profitability and survival of companies in each group.

The results provide a twist on the growth story in the more developed economies. While there was a strong correlation between top-line growth and TRS performance, there was a *weak* correlation between top-line growth and survival:

- High-growth companies had much higher TRS than low-growth companies: an average of 14 percent across the two business cycles, as against 2 percent for the slow growers.

- It was difficult to sustain high TRS performance without strong top-line growth. Two-thirds of the companies that turned in high TRS but low growth in the first business cycle were unable to sustain their TRS performance through to 2005.

- Low-growth companies were *not* more likely to exit; in fact, their survival rate was on a par with that of high-growth companies, at 86 and 85 percent respectively.[4]

We can attribute these distinctive findings to two main factors: the high growth rate of the Korean economy and a protective market that allowed weak corporations to survive. To understand their effects, we need to look back thirty years. During the 1970s, the domestic economy exhibited high growth of between 10 and 20 percent a year. Not all companies were growing at the same rate, but even slow-growing companies were likely to survive because they benefitted from overall industry growth (and low levels of competition). The corporate insolvency rate was very low: just 0.12 percent a year, compared to an average 0.85 percent in advanced economies.

At the same time, Korean companies were able to secure profits by operating in a well-protected domestic market and growing through exports. Government policies restricted imports (for instance, by confining tenders to domestic companies and levying high taxes on imported goods) and encouraged exports through tax and financial incentives (for instance, by ensuring banks offered favorable terms on loans to domestic companies).

Another factor that protected companies from the consequences of poor growth performance was Korea's relatively undeveloped capital and M&A markets, which meant they were unlikely to be subjected to aggressive acquisition or merger bids.

The origins of growth

To understand the strategies Korean companies adopted to grow over the two business cycles, we analyzed their performance at both the industry and company level and benchmarked it against the growth performance achieved by companies in other leading markets. We broke down growth into its three constituents:

- **Portfolio momentum:** growth dependent on the overall growth of the industry in which the company is competing.

- **M&A:** inorganic growth derived from mergers and acquisitions.

- **Market-share gain:** growth derived from share taken from competitors, independent of overall industry growth.

Most Korean companies followed a pattern that we can illustrate with reference to the country's leading industry, electronics. In the period 1999 to 2005, the electronics industry achieved rapid growth. The market leaders not only benefitted from the sector's growth but also gained market share from competitors at home and overseas. Though they made notable moves to enter new market segments, M&A played virtually no role in their growth, or in that of the industry as a whole.

Let's take a closer look at two of the market leaders, Samsung Electronics (SEC) and LG Electronics (LGE).

Founded in 1969, SEC started out as a white-goods manufacturer. After acquiring Korea Semiconductors in 1974, it was able to ride the tailwind of the semiconductors business. The fruits of this growth enabled SEC to develop its own technology independently and to produce a range of new products including 64K DRAM, 1M DRAM, and flash memory.

SEC grew at about 17 percent a year from 1999 to 2005. Half of this growth was attributable to the overall growth of the industry; the other half came from substantial market-share gains. All this growth was organic. Indeed, SEC's M&A activities led to negative growth when it divested three of its subsidiary businesses: optical-disk drives, its defense business, and its AST Research acquisition. Notably, much of SEC's growth was achieved outside its home market: it registered a CAGR of 20 to 30 percent in its overseas markets (including those of Asia and Europe), but only 3 percent in Korea.

In a nutshell, SEC seems to have been successful because it was in the right sector at the right time, invested in new technologies and products in its core business, and divested non-core businesses. Although its production and operations were domestic, it relied heavily on the overseas market for sales.

Much the same pattern is exhibited by LGE, which grew by 16.4 percent a year from 1999 to 2005. It generated half its growth from the overall growth of the industry and the other half from market-share gains (largely thanks to cost savings resulting from operational improvements). Like SEC, it carried out very little M&A.

In the high-tech industry, one exception to this pattern was SK Telecom, Korea's largest telecom operator. Originally, the SK Group's acquisition of newly privatized entities had helped it enter the telecommunications sector and record sizable inorganic growth during the period 1999 to 2005. Of its 16 percent overall growth, 5.6 percentage points came from its acquisition of Sinsegi Telecom and sale of SK Teletech.

On the whole though, few Korean companies use M&A as part of their growth strategy, regardless of the sector in which they compete. Take steel-refining, for instance. While POSCO recorded an average CAGR of 13 percent between 1999 and 2005, most of this derived from overall industry growth. The company undertook virtually no M&A. Nearly 70 percent of its current revenue is generated in the domestic market, where its growth has been closely tied to that of steel-consuming industries such as shipbuilding and the automotive sector.

The shipbuilding industry also experienced little inorganic growth in this period. One major player, DSME, grew by about 10 percent per year, largely as a result of overall industry growth.

Two sectors of Korean industry buck this general trend, however: automobiles and financial services.

The story is different in the auto industry where inorganic activity plays an important role in industry structure, conduct, and performance. Substantial consolidation has taken place over the past five years, with mergers between Kia and Hyundai, Ssangyong and SAIC, Samsung Auto and Renault, and Daewoo Auto and GM. Even so, organic growth is still by far the largest contributor to overall growth. Consider Hyundai, which achieved 12 percent annual growth during the period under review. With the exception of its acquisition of Kia Motors in early 2000, most of this growth derived from the expansion of the global car industry.

The financial sector represents the most dramatic departure from the general rule of organic growth in Korea. The reforms that followed the Asian financial crisis paved the way for consolidation in Korea's domestic banks. In the past ten years, the commercial banking industry has consolidated from more than 30 players to 15. The remaining players have grown strongly, with the market share of the top five banks increasing from 50 to more than 80 percent. At the company level, Shinhan's merger and acquisition of CHB and LG Card, for instance, produced more than two-thirds of its 35 percent CAGR over the past five years.

Overall, then, Korea's companies followed two main growth strategies in the two business cycles we examined. Most pursued organic growth exclusively, and concentrated on gaining market share in a particular business area. They channelled investment into developing new technologies and products and building local production facilities to serve global markets. A smaller number of companies combined organic growth with some domestic M&A, acquiring domestic competitors in the aftermath of the Asian financial crisis or former public entities on privatization. International M&A featured in neither of these strategies.

The evidence shows that Korean companies would much rather build than buy. When they do buy, they go for domestic opportunities.

Running out of steam

Will this approach to growth continue to serve Korea's companies well? We believe there are considerable doubts on this score.

If we turn first to purely organic strategies, there are three factors that may limit their effectiveness in future. The first is the shift in the management style of Korean corporations. The weakening of control in family-owned businesses as leadership passes from one generation to the next will inevitably militate against taking bold bets.

The second factor is the rising level of competition in Korea's domestic market. In the past, the high level of protection served to ensure good returns on large investments. However, newly endorsed free trade agreements allow foreign companies full access to Korea's markets. So far, Korea has signed such agreements with Singapore, six European countries, the US, and Chile. It is in active discussions with the EU, ASEAN, Canada, Mexico, and India, and is keen to pursue an agreement with China. Clearly, Korea's companies will soon be exposed to far more competition from foreign players with much less protection than they had in the past.

Finally, Korea's corporations are facing increasing pressures on their cost competitiveness. Rises in the foreign exchange rate, in labor costs, and in transportation and logistics costs all threaten Korea's attractiveness as a global production base, especially in comparison with China. While Korea's manufacturing costs have risen over the past ten years and now equate to 80 percent of the US level, China's manufacturing costs remain at just 20 to 30 percent of Korea's.

There are challenges for the hybrid approach combining organic growth with domestic M&A as well. Acquisition targets are becoming increasingly scarce. Many domestic sectors have already reached their optimal level of consolidation or are close to doing so. The past five years have seen significant consolidation in the financial sector, the semiconductor industry, and the automotive sector. In most key industries, such as retail distribution, ship-building, automotive, electronics, and banking, the top three companies now account for nearly 60 percent of the market.

Fresh options for growth
So what avenues are left for Korean companies seeking growth? We have identified three options for them to consider.

Capture remaining domestic M&A opportunities
Although many industry sectors are close to being fully concentrated and so present limited opportunities for M&A, a thorough search can sometimes reveal hidden opportunities. For example, there are still a number of entities

awaiting sale that were rescued by the government after the Asian financial crisis through an injection of public funds. The list includes Daewoo Inc., Woori Bank, DSME, and Daewoo Securities.

Another set of opportunities lies with entities awaiting privatization. Some companies have already reaped the rewards of acquiring privatized companies, as SKT has done with its acquisition of Sinsegi and Korea Mobile Telecommunications. Of the entities on the current list, KEPCO and IBK could present attractive opportunities once privatized.

Companies looking for growth should also bear in mind the impact regulatory changes are likely to have on industry structures. The securities sector, for instance, is expected to undergo significant consolidation after the enactment of the Capital Market Consolidation Act. The insurance industry is also awaiting long-term restructuring.

For mid-sized conglomerates encumbered with portfolios of low-growth businesses, such opportunities may present their only real hope of boosting their growth rate. They will certainly yield returns more readily than other strategies such as expanding overseas or investing in completely new business arenas.

M&A can also act as a route to corporate transformation. Until the end of the 1990s, the Doosan Group focused on OB Beer, with a portfolio in advertising, packaging, and bottle manufacture built in support of its core business. So when the company sold off its beer operations, its growth could easily have been jeopardized. However, Doosan used the proceeds from the sale to reinvent itself by acquiring Korea Heavy Industry in 2000, Daewoo Heavy Industry in 2005, and more recently Bobcat in the US.

Build a global footprint and master global operations

As long as domestic growth sticks at around 4 percent a year, the relatively small size of Korea's domestic market will make it difficult to achieve high growth at home. The answer is to look overseas.

If Korean companies are to succeed in new international markets, they will need to abandon their traditional approach to expansion, namely locating production in Korea and then exporting overseas. This model relied on two conditions that no longer apply: a protected domestic market and the price-competitiveness of Korean products in overseas markets. Instead, companies will need to adopt a new model in which R&D, production, and sales are optimized to achieve scale on a global basis. This calls for a truly global perspective in which world markets are viewed in their entirety.

The auto industry already operates in this manner. The top five global manufacturers now account for more than 70 percent of the world market. Strategies are shaped at a global rather than local or regional level.

Viewed from this perspective, M&A becomes an important tool for securing revenue growth in fast-growing overseas markets such as India, China, and eastern Europe. Organic growth is seldom an option for late entrants in such markets. Consider retail, for instance: it is now some 20 years since Wal-Mart and Carrefour first set foot in the Chinese market, and it would be a tall order for Korea's retailers to succeed there today by opening new branches from scratch. M&A offers a more viable route in retail, as it does in the financial and banking industries. Indeed, any CEO thinking globally will need to have M&A on his or her agenda.

Create new businesses to meet emerging customer needs

The third option for Korean companies is to identify tomorrow's growth engines: those businesses that satisfy the needs of new and emerging customer segments. To find them, companies will need to take a granular view of the market. To capture them, companies will need the ability to stay a step ahead of the competition and the flexibility to shift their resources to meet newly identified demands.

Where can companies find these new market opportunities? One good starting point is to look at long-term trends. Korea has one of the most rapidly aging populations of any society in the world, for instance. New growth opportunities will emerge at a granular level over the next decade or two in such areas as welfare, pensions, health insurance, healthcare, and leisure and travel services.

Another long-term trend likely to open up new market opportunities is that of increasing environmental challenges. Within 20 years, water will become one of the most precious natural resources. Since Korea is short of water, businesses such as water purification and bottled-water supply are likely to offer avenues for growth.

Speed is of the essence, however. If opportunities exist, chances are that someone else has spotted them too. Korean companies have already moved into the water business, for instance. The Kolon Group aspires to be one of the world's top 10 water companies by 2015, when it hopes to generate more than US$2 billion in revenues from that sector. It has already succeeded in acquiring Environment Facilities Management Corporation, Korea's biggest sewage disposal company, in a competitive bid against Veolia, France's largest water business.

Where to start

If Korean companies are to pursue these growth opportunities, they will need to take three main steps.

Reshape the business portfolio

Companies need to view their portfolio objectively. A company stuck in a low-growth industry needs to establish where the next growth tailwind will come from and move its business accordingly. But this is no place for a broad-brush approach; executives will need to view their industry in a granular way if they are to uncover pockets of growth. The telecoms industry may have attractive overall growth rates, for example, but the fixed-line business holds out little promise of growth over the next few years.

Companies also need to take a long hard look at their industry to understand the scale of the potential it offers. If the result of this scrutiny is disappointing, they will need to move to find a new core business, most likely via M&A. Here they will face two main challenges.

The first is funding: most Korean conglomerates are constrained by the nature of their ownership structure and the regulatory imposition of a 25 percent ceiling on total equity. This makes it difficult for them to pursue M&A while retaining management control. To be able to snatch up acquisition opportunities as they become available, they need a more flexible governance structure. Some Korean companies, such as LG, SK, and Dongwon, are already moving from a circular ownership structure to a holding company structure.

The second challenge faced by Korean companies pursuing M&A lies in building the capabilities for managing a business after acquisition.

Identify the right globalization model

Most companies in Korea agree that globalization is the most important topic on their CEO's agenda. What this means for their company isn't always clear, however.

The term "globalization" is sometimes used too glibly. Companies should bear in mind that its impact varies greatly from sector to sector. While automobile and semiconductor manufacture are genuinely global industries with huge global players, that isn't the case in, say, real estate, education, food, and household goods, where tastes and demand are still defined at a national or regional level. When executives think about "What is the likely impact of globalization on my business?" or "What do I need to do to respond to globalization?" they need to do so in a granular fashion, basing their deliberations on the specific characteristics of the sectors and sub-sectors where they operate.

Put in place a global management system

When a Korean company acquires a foreign company, the CEO's biggest concern is likely to be "How do I manage the company after I acquire it?" This is hardly surprising given that few CEOs – even those that have run overseas branches or subsidiaries – have had much experience of managing locals. Samsung Electronics is typical of most Korean companies with overseas interests in that its foreign subsidiaries are largely run by executives sent out from Korea. But this is not an approach that can be sustained when companies make large-scale acquisitions. If a Korean business is to thrive in the local market of a newly acquired company, it will have to adapt its organization and management to the culture and language of the country concerned.

Few Korean companies possess a well-defined system for managing overseas companies as yet. They will need to co-ordinate decision making between their overseas subsidiaries and their Korean headquarters by putting in place clear standards in reporting and procedures. Another hurdle for most Korean companies is the size of their global talent pool. They need executives who are fluent in English, capable of adapting to different cultures, and able to make business decisions from a top-management perspective.

Building effective governance structures and developing and securing talent will take time. Companies seeking to grow overseas would be advised to start now rather than wait until later.

■ ■ ■

Korean companies are at a crossroads. The strategies they pursued through the good old days of high growth will no longer serve them well. It is time to choose a different path. Their success, and that of the economy as a whole, will depend on how well they adapt to new circumstances and whether they are able to discover new growth tailwinds. The next five or six years will be critical in determining whether they will grow or go.

NOTES

[1] Sven Smit, Caroline Thompson, and Patrick Viguerie, "The do-or-die struggle for growth," *The McKinsey Quarterly*, 2005 number 3, pp. 35–45.

[2] These 60 companies represented almost two-thirds of Korea's entire GDP in 1993.

[3] Nine of the original 60 companies had disappeared during the second cycle.

[4] Going bankrupt and being bought out both count as exiting.

The authors

Jonathan Auerbach is the managing partner of McKinsey's Southeast Asia practice, which spans offices in Singapore, Thailand, Malaysia, Indonesia, and the Philippines. During the 1980s and 1990s, he was responsible for McKinsey's telecom and high-tech practices in Asia. He has worked extensively with clients across Asia, Europe, and the US in telecom, technology, multimedia, and entertainment.

Wonsik Choi is a principal in McKinsey's Seoul office and a member of the leadership team for the Asia-Pacific strategy practice. He helps companies to develop a vision and strategy and to undertake major transformation programs. He is an expert on risk management, building new businesses, and integration.

Angus Dawson is a principal in McKinsey's Sydney office and leads the growth initiative of the Asia-Pacific strategy practice. Over the past ten years, he has worked with large companies in a range of industries to help them grow. His work focuses on corporate strategy, business-unit strategy, and organization design.

Carl Harris is an associate principal in McKinsey's Singapore office and a member of the Asian telecom and principal investors' practice. Over the past seven years, he has helped companies and investors across Europe, Asia, and Africa to address issues of strategy, corporate finance, and growth.

Kuldeep Jain is an associate principal in McKinsey's Mumbai office. He helps domestic companies to create globalization strategies and conduct cross-border deals, and assists multinational corporations in evaluating, closing, and integrating India acquisitions and making cross-border mergers and acquisitions.

Peter Kenevan is a principal in McKinsey's Tokyo office and a leader of the corporate finance practice. He works primarily with high-tech and retail companies and advises them on issues such as mergers and acquisition strategies and the corporate finance agenda.

Sangbeom Kim is an associate principal in McKinsey's Seoul office and a member of the Asia-Pacific strategy, retail, and financial institutions practices. He works with clients on issues of corporate strategy and governance, corporate finance, risk management, product development, and leadership enhancement.

Gordon Orr is a director in McKinsey's Shanghai office. He led the Greater China practice for many years and is now head of the Asian strategy practice. He helps clients identify and solve strategy, partnership, and related organization challenges and is an expert on alliances between Chinese and international businesses.

Vivek Pandit is a principal in McKinsey's Mumbai office and the leader of the corporate finance, high-tech, media, and telecom practices in India. He works with companies across India, China, Japan, and Korea on growth, M&A, operations, and organization.

Herbert Pohl is a principal in McKinsey's Dubai office and leads the corporate finance practice in the Middle East. He works with clients on CFO-related topics including finance, operations, performance management, and IPO/privatizations.

Adil Zainulbhai is the managing partner of McKinsey's India practice. Based in the Mumbai office, he helps Indian companies to become successful globally. He has worked with large companies to develop telecom strategies and helped venture-funded start-ups in the telecom and wireless industries.

Index